W9-AKV-984

TRUTH FOR LIFE®

THE BIBLE-TEACHING MINISTRY OF **ALISTAIR BEGG**

The mission of Truth For Life is to teach the Bible with clarity and relevance so that unbelievers will be converted, believers will be established, and local churches will be strengthened.

Daily Program

Each day, Truth For Life distributes the Bible teaching of Alistair Begg across the U.S. and in several locations outside of the U.S. through 2,000 radio outlets. To find a radio station near you, visit **truthforlife.org/stationfinder**.

Free Teaching

The daily program, and Truth For Life's entire teaching library of over 3,000 Bible-teaching messages, can be accessed for free online at **truthforlife.org** and through Truth For Life's mobile app, which can be downloaded for free from your app store.

At-Cost Resources

Books and audio studies from Alistair Begg are available for purchase at cost, with no markup. Visit **truthforlife.org/store**.

Where to Begin?

If you're new to Truth For Life and would like to know where to begin listening and learning, find starting point suggestions at **truthforlife.org/firststep**. For a full list of ways to connect with Truth For Life, visit **truthforlife.org/subscribe**.

Contact Truth For Life

P.O. Box 398000 Cleveland, Ohio 44139
phone 1 (888) 588-7884   **email** letters@truthforlife.org
truthforlife.org

KNOWABLE WORD

HELPING ORDINARY PEOPLE LEARN TO STUDY THE BIBLE

(Revised and Expanded Edition)

Peter Krol

For Ben Hagerup,
who first showed me
how exciting Bible study could be.

CruciformPress

"Peter Krol has done us a great service by writing the book *Knowable Word*. It is valuable for those who have never done in-depth Bible study and a good review for those who have. **I look forward to using this book to improve my own Bible study.**"

Jerry Bridges, author and speaker (d. 2016)

"At the heart of *Knowable Word* is a glorious and crucial conviction: that understanding the Bible is not the preserve of a few, but the privilege and joy of all God's people. **Peter Krol's book demystifies the process of reading God's Word and in so doing enfranchises the people of God.** I warmly encourage you to read it. Better still, read it with others and apply its method together."

Dr. Tim Chester, The Porterbrook Network

"**Here is an excellent practical guide to interpreting the Bible.** Krol has thought through, tested, and illustrated in a clear, accessible way basic steps in interpreting the Bible, and made everything available in a way that will encourage ordinary people to deepen their own study."

Vern Poythress, Professor of New Testament Interpretation, Westminster Theological Seminary

"This book has three primary virtues and many secondary ones. Its primary virtues are the nobility of its goal (to equip Christians to interpret and apply the Bible), the accuracy of the proposed methodology for interacting with the Bible, and the practical approach to the subject. Additionally, *Knowable Word* book does a splendid job of employing the practice of 'learning by doing.'"

Leland Ryken, Emeritus Professor of English at Wheaton College and author of *How to Read the Bible as Literature*

"Peter Krol has written a book that many will find helpful in studying the Bible. Not just new believers, but anyone who wants to think about Scripture will find much here that strengthens their ability to read, study, understand, and apply the biblical text. Illuminating illustrations, helpful examples, and good exercises make this **a good, solid tool** that might be best used in a small group that is either starting to study Scripture together, or that wants to become better readers of the Bible. **A book to be recommended, read, and used.**"

Frederic Clarke Putnam, Ph.D., Associate Professor of Biblical Studies, The Templeton Honors College at Eastern University (St. Davids, PA).

"The Word of God is a feast laid before us. Yet we should be concerned with the Church's growing inability to enjoy this feast. If we don't know the Bible, we won't know the God of the Bible, either. *Knowable Word* does a tremendous service. It gives us tools to dig into the Bible that go far beyond the most common light and superficial methods. **This book is biblically rooted, theologically rich, time-tested, and extremely applicable.** Read and use it in your own study, and give it to others in your life and ministry. Enjoy the feast!"

Stephen Lutz, pastor, and author of *King of the Campus* and *College Ministry in a Post-Christian Culture*

Don't miss this companion volume from Peter Krol

Sowable Word: Helping Ordinary People
Learn to **Lead Bible Studies**

Knowable Word: Helping Ordinary People Learn to Study the Bible
(Revised and Expanded Edition)

Print / PDF ISBN: 978-1-949253-33-7
ePub ISBN: 978-1-949253-35-1
Mobipocket ISBN: 978-1-949253-34-4

Contents

Foreword

The Bible is a treasure. The infinite God has communicated truth to finite creatures, and he has done so in human language, not celestial. In the Bible we have truth in a fixed form, in words that read the same from day to day. God has revealed all the truth we must understand to live in his world; we are not left to our own devices.

The Bible is objective. We need not derive truth through subjective spiritual impressions. God has revealed truth in an objective form. He has revealed Himself with words; words written down by men who were inspired by the Holy Spirit and kept from error as they wrote. (2 Peter 1:20–21).

The Bible is a revelation of absolute truth. The only way finite humans can have absolute truth is by revelation. All human knowledge is subject to constant revision. More study, additional information, and new discoveries must be collated and incorporated to continually reshape what is known. Human knowledge always has a tentative quality. Thus, there is a non-permanence to human knowledge. Not so with the Bible. God has infinite knowledge. He knows all things real, all things possible, and all things potential. Since God has infinite knowledge he can, and has, revealed absolute truth. In the Scripture we have a limited revelation of truth (we don't know everything that could be known), truth that will always be true (it will never prove false or unreliable), and truth that is sufficient (it is all the truth we will ever need). What a treasure!

Since God used words to give us a book of absolute truth, truth we need to know and understand—what could be more important than understanding this book? Sadly, many Christian people see the Bible as a confusing book shrouded in mystery and requiring some secret insight if it is to be understood. No wonder so few really study it. No wonder it is sometimes read as a religious exercise rather than as the life-giving treasure it truly is.

That's what *Knowable Word* is all about. The Word of God is knowable. Christians can learn simple steps that will enable them to understand and inwardly digest the Word of God and be transformed by its truth.

In *Knowable Word*, Krol introduces and develops three methods for unlocking the meaning of any passage of Scripture. 1) Observation—what does it say? 2) Interpretation—what does it mean? 3) Application—how should I change? Throughout the book Krol opens and expands on this straightforward and memorable method for knowing God's Word. He tells us what to observe, how to find the right interpretation, and suggests ways in which we must make application. In each of these steps the reader is given an easy-to-remember framework for keeping all the pieces in order.

Knowable Word is especially valuable because it is field-tested. Peter Krol has been teaching this approach to Bible study for years. He teaches these things to university students as a DiscipleMakers staff and to ordinary people in the pew as an elder in Christ's church. Each audience, though diverse in life-stage, education, and age, is able to track with this teaching. Krol brings clarity and ease of communication to understanding the Bible. This book possesses the rare quality of being simple without being shallow. It is at once accessible and yet profound and challenging.

I had the joy of seeing Peter teach this material in the church I served as pastor for twenty-nine years. The illustrations used in teaching were from the Proverbs, but the same method was employed—observation, interpretation, and application. In reading this book I was struck with how clearly the methods of understanding the text worked even though the passage under consideration was different.

When Krol taught this method of Bible study to our congregation, people came alive as each step unfolded. They found themselves able to make observations, which they would not have made without these categories, from which to frame their observations. I witnessed their excitement as they made observations that made sense of the text under consideration. I saw the smiles that said, "Hey, I can do this." The reader of *Knowable Word* will have the same experience.

The same was true with interpreting. Krol provides neat, accessible ways of asking questions that aid in the process of interpretation. These questions lead to interpretive conclusions. Again the class was abuzz with the excitement of more ideas than could be adequately entertained during the limited class time.

The time spent in observation and interpretation led seamlessly to application for our Sunday school class. The class was given simple, memorable ways of thinking about how Scripture maps on to life. It was practical application that impacted our thinking; what we should think, how we should feel, and what we should do.

Woven through this book, Krol has placed timely *Your Turn* exercises to enable the reader to practice what is being learned. These exercises take the content of the book out of the theoretical and into the practical.

It is hard to over-estimate the value of this tidy volume. It is clear and uncomplicated. No one will be off-put by this book. It will engage the novice and the serious student of Scripture. It works as a solid read for individuals or as an exciting study for a small group, whether old or young.

Since "All Scripture is breathed out by God and profitable for teaching, for reproof, for correction, and for training in righteousness, that the man of God may be competent, equipped for every good work" (2 Timothy 3:16–17) , it is my prayer that this little volume will be richly blessed by God to the edification of his saints.

Tedd Tripp

Preface
to the Second Edition

As a guitarist, I used to have a joke with fellow guitarists. How do you ever get a guitarist to stop playing his guitar? Put real sheet music—not merely chord charts—in front of him! That joke has become a parable of sorts for my ministry of helping people learn to study the Bible. That's because, sadly, people with Bibles don't always know how to use them. They know how to collect study guides, commentaries, sermon audio, study Bibles, lecture notes, magazines, blog feeds, and inspiring quotes. They're good at absorbing and repeating what they're taught. They know how to read the "chord charts."

But the average Christian alone with a Bible is as helpless as the average guitarist stuck with real sheet music.

Now don't get me wrong: Study guides are a crucial part of Christian education. Their role in Bible study is like that of a tee in the sport of baseball.

The tee is the first guidepost for children learning to play the sport. It assures young athletes that they can hit the ball and not fear it will hit them. It defines where to stand, where to swing the bat, and when to run. It's a good friend and capable mentor.

As those athletes develop, the tee endures as a tool. Even the pros use tees to help them perfect the mechanics of batting. However, *the tee is not part of the big game*. While the tee trains and refines, it prepares players for the game of baseball, and then it gets out of the way.

In the same way, decent study guides shape Bible students. They assist young Christians in practicing the basics. They embolden new leaders by providing a ready-made structure for discussion groups. They develop mature believers by honing their understanding of Scripture and keeping them connected with the insights of others.

But this book will help you learn to play the game without a tee. It will help you learn to study the Bible for yourself.

Who Is This Book For?

The Reformation and its offspring put Bibles in the hands of ordinary people, but these hands are often clumsy in their craft. So explanatory materials have multiplied, fueling in the hearts of God's people an increasing fervor for God's word. And God willing, this fervor will never abate. If you are among those who share this fervor, this book is for you.

1. Are you a beginner who loves God and his word? Perhaps you see others draw close to God through his word, and you want in on it. You faithfully attend church services, but you're certain you could never do what the pastor or leader does. So you keep listening and watching. You'd be delighted to experience richer insight; you just don't know where to start.

2. Are you a mature Christian who wants to internalize your Bible study skills? Churches are full of people who have a daily quiet time with their Bible, journal, and *workbook* or *study guide*. These folks have experienced some decent Bible study, and they pretty much get the basics. But they want to be able to do it on their own. Does this describe you? You're used to riding with training wheels, but you're itching to pop them off, let loose, and just keep pedaling.

3. Are you a leader who longs not only to teach but also to equip? You have an effective ministry. People come to Christ. People grow in Christ. People lead others to Christ and engage their communities. The church or small group thrives. But the ministry centers on you, the leader. People come to you with questions; they get answers and go on their way. You desire a better legacy for the Lord—one that produces disciple-making disciples—but you don't quite know how to reproduce yourself. You do what you do instinctively, and you're not sure how to package it up for wholesale distribution.

Who Has Used This Book?

I first wrote *Knowable Word* to take what we do in our campus ministry with DiscipleMakers (www.dm.org) and package it up for others to benefit from. Since the book's publication, I have been delighted to hear from a number of people I expected would benefit from it—especially pastors, small group leaders, and Sunday school teachers.

But I've also heard from others whom I wouldn't have predicted to be within reach of this book. A missionary, who has been training indigenous pastors of underground churches for nearly two decades, tells me he now uses the book for coaching those church leaders. An attorney tells me he's distributed copies among families in his fellowship. An 89-year-old man writes to say it's helped his mentoring of his nephew. And a southeast Asian teenager sends his thanks for helping him to better understand the Lord's Book, which has pointed him more clearly to Jesus.

The most common category of folks who have contacted me about the book have been youth pastors. I did not write *Knowable Word* with teenagers in mind, but the Lord has for some reason seen fit to use it in support of youth ministry in various parts of the world. And I couldn't be more grateful. My own church (Grace Fellowship Church of State College, PA) has the following as one of its objectives in children's ministry:

> *To encourage and model to the middle school*
> *and high school children how to spend time with*
> *God in his Word and prayer and to teach them*
> *how to study and apply the Word for themselves*
> *by learning and practicing OIA through various*
> *books of the Bible. To give them opportunities*
> *to study a subject topically so they can begin to*
> *understand the whole counsel of God about*
> *questions they or their friends may have.*

If this book helps other churches in some small ways to develop a similar vision for discipling their young people, I couldn't be more thrilled.

What Has Changed in the Second Edition?

In addition to improving the prose in various ways, this second edition expands substantially on the topics of structure, context, and literary form (which now includes not only what the first edition called "genre" but also a new concept called "text type"). In the years since the first edition was published, I have come to a deeper understanding of each of these concepts and what role each plays in the OIA method. Structure has become, in my opinion, one of the most important things to observe, as it, more than any other observation, surfaces the contours of not only the artistry but also the very *argument* the author seeks to make. Context really matters; without an eye for it, Bible readers are prone to go in so many different directions, which would likely have been unrecognizable to the Bible's original authors. And text type provides a complement to genre, as a parallel way to view a text's literary form; in fact, I've found that text type often provides students an even more useful set of tools than those provided by observing the genre.

I've also given more specific steps to help you follow an author's train of thought, identify the weightiest segment of a passage, and thereby be more likely to discover the author's main point. In my personal training of others, I find the greatest challenge for most is to gain a healthy suspicion of their familiarity with the text so they might learn how to truly observe it. But once that milestone has been reached, the next most difficult skill is determining the author's main point. Our ability to perceive that main point requires us to know how to think and how to follow an argument. So I've expanded the instruction at that point to help you master these crucial skills.

What Almost Changed in the Second Edition?

The most frequent feedback I have received on the book is the request for an "answer key" to the *Your Turn* exercises found throughout the book. To date, I have staunchly refused providing one to any inquirer on the ground that the act of providing my own answer key would undermine the entire purpose of helping *you* gain the confidence you need to study the Bible for yourself and to believe you are approved to do so.

However, I have become persuaded that the climb — from *spectator* of my ongoing demonstration of the OIA method with Genesis 1 to *practitioner* of the self-guided study questions for Genesis 2 — is a bit too steep for those who have never before tried this at home. So I have decided to now let people know how I would answer the questions I pose in those *Your Turn* exercises.

But I will do so only if you promise not to view those answers as the only "right" answers. And if you don't look at those answers until you've first tried to answer the questions for yourself. I offer them not as an authoritative or impeccable way to study Genesis 2:4–25, but simply as a potential measuring rod by which you can evaluate whether you're on the right track in practicing the skills laid out in this book.

That is why the answer key "almost" changed in the second edition. You won't find it in this book. I couldn't make it too easy for you to flip right from the exercises themselves to my guidance on the exercises, could I? If you would like to read my answers to the *Your Turn* exercises, you'll have to first try them yourself. Then if you want to see if you're on the right track, you can visit the blog at *www.knowableword.com/resources* and find the Guidance for *Your Turn* Exercises. It wasn't ordained by angels in the hand of a mediator or anything like that, but perhaps it will provide some suitable help and courage.

Now, are you ready to begin? May every word of God prove true, as he proves to be a shield to those who take refuge in him (Proverbs 30:5).

One

Why Study the Bible?

Unpacking Scripture Rightly

In my home office, there's a fireproof safe where my wife and I keep our most precious possessions. There are the expected legal papers, but mostly we've filled it with the forty-five love letters that document the development of our romance. This bundle of letters is more than a collection of mementos; it's our story.

The story begins with a question mark.

A love-struck young man composes a poetic thank-you note to a sweet girl who has done a nice thing for him. He ends the note with a simple question—a question clear enough to give her reason to write back, but vague enough to prevent any guilt should she choose not to.

But she does write back, asking her own vague question in return.

This is it! Queen's knight to c3. Game on…

The remaining details must remain private, but I'll share this much: we pored over every letter we received. We wrapped our hearts in them, squeezing every juicy jot and tittle for its last drop of meaning. We didn't read these letters because we had to, though there was some sense of compulsion. We didn't read them primarily to learn about one another, though it's true each letter brought more information. We did more than read them. We fixated on them, indulged in them, absorbed them. Through it all, we sought one thing: to get to know each other. We each knew there was someone behind the text, a person we desperately wanted to know. So we read—and did more than read—because we wanted a relationship.

You see where I'm going with this, right? You and I have the Bible as an absolutely indispensable help in building our relationships with the God who wrote it. He already knows us perfectly, and he wants us to know him better and better. He became a man to reconcile us to himself and live with us forever, and he left a book documenting the whole affair. "And this is eternal life, that they know you the only true God, and Jesus Christ whom you have sent" (John 17:3).

But do you really know how to dig into that book? Most of us know how to collect study guides, commentaries, sermon audio, study Bibles, lecture notes, magazines, blog feeds, and inspiring quotes—stuff *about* the Bible. We're good at absorbing and repeating what we're taught—what we heard *someone else say* about the Bible. But most of us don't know how to dig into the Bible itself, mine its endless seam of precious gems, and come away spiritually richer and more in love with the awesome God who has given us his only Son as our Lord and Savior.

Now don't get me wrong: Bible study guides are a crucial part of Christian education. They represent a non-threatening way to get started in Bible study, a limited approximation of the real thing. So, while they can be a great step in the right direction, they are not the destination. In the same way, quality study guides can help shape Bible students. They assist young Christians in practicing the basics. They embolden new leaders by providing a ready-made structure for discussion groups. They develop mature believers by honing their understanding of Scripture and keeping them connected with the insights of others.

But this book is different. Its primary purpose is not to tell you what the Bible says, and with few exceptions it will not serve up gems mined by others. Instead, it will point you to the seam, hand you the tools you'll need, and teach you the best way to extract the endless riches of Scripture. It will help you learn to study the Bible for yourself, and thus know better the God who gave us his Word to make himself known.

No Celestial Choirs Needed

Sometimes we think we need a special encounter to know God. We seek a mountaintop experience where we can behold his glory and see him face to face. We want to hear his voice speaking with clarity and power.

We long to be wowed from on high. The apostle Peter had such an experience with Jesus, and he concluded that you and I don't need to have the same experience.

> We were eyewitnesses of his majesty. For when he received honor and glory from God the Father, and the voice was borne to him by the Majestic Glory, "This is my beloved Son, with whom I am well pleased," we ourselves heard this very voice borne from heaven, for we were with him on the holy mountain. And we have the prophetic word *more fully confirmed*, to which you will do well to pay attention as to a lamp shining in a dark place. (2 Peter 1:16b–19a)

Peter loved the mountaintop. There's nothing wrong with the mountaintop. But don't miss Peter's larger point—we don't *need* the mountaintop to know God; what we *need* is to pay very close attention to the Word God has already spoken. *That* is where he speaks with the greatest clarity and the most authoritative power.

This is why, when Paul wanted to introduce people to Jesus, he introduced them to the Bible (Acts 17:1–3). Since the whole Bible is about Jesus (John 1:45, 5:39–40; Luke 24:44–49; 1 Peter 1:10–12), we likewise can meet him there.

In short, we study the Bible to know Jesus and to help others know him.

Maybe you've never studied the Bible without a tour guide or commentary, and you'd like to learn the basics. Perhaps you know the basics but want to make them instinctive, like an athlete perfecting a skill through constant repetition. Or perhaps you already teach the Bible, but you do so intuitively, unsure of how to take what you do and package it up for whole-sale distribution among your flock.

Whatever your situation may be, a simple, sensible Bible study method will help. This book offers such a method, but first, guess what? You already have a Bible study method.

Everyone Has a Bible Study Method

How do you respond to the word *method*? Does it make you nervous, or is it a relief? Does it make you feel like you're in a laboratory? Does it resurface bad memories of rules, rules, and more rules from your upbringing? Or does it inspire you with the promise of clarity and direction?

Whatever your reaction, I propose that *every-one* has one or more Bible study methods. Most of these are *unintentional* and *informal*. Here are some examples.

The Divination Method: Open the Bible… flip through it until something strikes you… read what you find… trust this is God's will for you today.

The Support Group Method: Read a passage of the Bible… close the Bible… consider (or discuss, if in a group situation) how you feel about what you just read.

The Prayerful Method: Ask God to bring to mind a passage of the Bible that will address your current problem or need… listen to what thoughts come into your mind… look at those passages for encouragement or help.

Other methods are quite *intentional* and *formal*.

The Cross-Reference Method: Read a passage of the Bible… look up another passage that this one reminds you of… look up a third passage that the second one reminds you of… look up a fourth passage that the third one reminds you of… repeat until exhausted.

The Word Study Method: Decide which topic you'd like to study in the Bible… identify one or more key words that represent your topic… search the Bible for passages that use those key words… read each verse that comes up… compile the teaching of all the verses into a unified whole… live in light of what you learned.

The Expert Method: Read a chosen passage of the Bible… read study notes or a commentary on that passage of the Bible… believe and act upon what the commentator wrote.

If the Bible is important to you, you have almost certainly used at least a few of these methods, and probably have a favorite one. The problem is that *not every method is a good one.* Many of the most popular methods don't (and can't) result in correct interpretation. If God wrote the Bible so we'd know Jesus, shouldn't we make sure we're understanding what we read?

OIA: Unpacking the Bible Rightly

This book is all about a very old Bible study method that has had many names,[1] but today often uses the acronym OIA:

1. Observation—what does it say?

2. Interpretation—what does it mean?

3. Application—how should I change?

You can restate these three steps as "what," "why," and "so what." Or again, as "what the original author said," "what that meant to the original audience," and "what it means in our context."[2]

The OIA method has many benefits. It teaches us to hear the text and respond to it. It trains us in critical thinking and clear communication. It interests postdocs, preschoolers, and everyone in between. It can be learned in five minutes and perfected over a lifetime.

The other methods I mentioned aren't completely wrong, but most of them focus on one skill (observation, interpretation, or application) exclusively. But consider what happens if we miss any part of the OIA process.

If we neglect good *observation* of the text, our service to Christ can easily launch off in the wrong direction. We love him and want to know him, but we're like homebuilders who ignore the blueprint and trash the work order: we end up with "interesting" houses not up to code and possibly unsafe to live in.

If we neglect good *interpretation* of the text, our beliefs and actions will likely be unbiblical. We will end up like homebuilders who have constructed a geothermally heated yacht, completely missing the designer's intention.

If we neglect good *application* of the text (how we ought to change), we might be wasting our time altogether. We can be like foolish builders founding a home upon sand (Matthew 7:26–27). We build it, but since no one can live in it for long, nothing really changes.

Why OIA is the Best Method

There are three reasons why I'm convinced that the substance behind the OIA method of Bible study represents the best of all possible approaches.

OIA Describes How All Communication Works

OIA is neither new nor innovative. It simply outlines the steps by which all human beings communicate with each other—we observe what was communicated, we interpret the meaning, and we respond (and when all goes well, we respond appropriately). God designed communication to work this way, so our Bible study should follow this universal pattern.

For example, if you see me in public, you might *observe* me as I approach, smile, and stick out my right hand. You would *interpret* that I mean you no harm and want to greet you. You would *apply* the interaction by reaching out your own hand, taking my hand with yours, and saying, "Hello." Communication has now taken place.

Or let's say I ask you a question. You might *observe* the higher inflection at the end of the sentence (the audible question mark), a resultant silence, and raised eyebrows. You would *interpret* these signs to mean that I want you to answer the question. You would *apply* your conclusion by answering the question, frowning in thought, holding up a finger to request more time, or ignoring me altogether.

You cannot escape OIA. You do it all the time. The OIA method helps you to make explicit what is implicit in any form of communication. It's how you figure out anything, really. Why not use it when studying the Bible?

OIA Works for Any Person, Anywhere, of Any Age

The OIA method merely codifies what all communicators do intuitively. Thus, Sunday schools can teach this method to young children. Everyday people like you and me can employ it in our quiet times. Bible scholars can use it to sharpen their insights and evaluate competing interpretations. Cross-cultural missionaries can use it in the field.

OIA Summarizes Jesus' Approach to the Bible

Jesus is the Lord, and his Spirit is the author of Scripture (1 Peter 1:11), so we should learn our Bible study method from him. See here how he corrects the Pharisees.

> Jesus said to them, "Have you never read in the Scriptures: 'The stone that the builders rejected has become the cornerstone; this was the Lord's doing, and it is marvelous in our eyes'? [43] Therefore I tell you, the kingdom of God will be taken away from you and given to a people producing its fruits. [44] And the one who falls on this stone will be broken to pieces; and when it falls on anyone, it will crush him." (Matthew 21:42–44)

First, Jesus draws his critics' attention to Psalm 118. This *observation* of the Old Testament text hits hard, since Jesus' two prior parables (Matthew 21:28–41) made clear that the chief priests and Pharisees are like the builders who rejected the cornerstone (Matthew 21:45). Second, Jesus *interprets* the psalm in verse 43, asserting that God will take the kingdom away from them and give it to others who bear the fruits of faith. Finally, Jesus *applies* the psalm in verse 44, offering the chief priests and Pharisees a stark choice: either "fall on Jesus and be broken, or wait for him to come in judgment and crush them."[3]

Jesus often references Scripture, but he's rarely as overt as in Matthew 21:42–44. Usually he assumes or implies the interpretation and states the observation and application explicitly (see Matthew 13:10–17 or Mark 12:35–37). One place he observes and interprets, but expects his audience to apply, is Luke 4:17–21. But note this well: *whenever Jesus references an Old Testament text, he uses the OIA process.*

In asserting that OIA is the best Bible study method, I'm not suggesting there's an easy one-size-fits-all way of plugging every text into an equation. But I am proposing there's a clear and valuable method by which you can understand what God is communicating in his Word.

Your study of the Bible should not be arbitrary. Don't allow poor methods to keep you from knowing Jesus better.

Your Turn

1. Pay attention the next time you communicate with another person. Try to identify the observation, interpretation, and application.
2. Read and consider Matthew 13:10–17. What passage does Jesus quote? How does he observe the text? How does he apply the text? What is his assumed interpretation?
3. Read and consider Mark 12:35–37. What passage does Jesus quote? How does he observe the text? How does he apply the text? What is his assumed interpretation?

4. Read and consider Luke 4:17–21. What passage does Jesus quote? How does he observe the text? How does he interpret the text? What is his assumed application?

We Need God's Spirit to Study the Bible

We must not expect God to grant complete—or even adequate—knowledge of himself without some hard work on our part. Our Lord wants us to pursue him with heart, mind, and strength, and he delights to meet us when we make that effort. At the same time, our faith is never to be in how well we understand and implement a process, because then our faith would be in our own mastery of a technique. Remember that our sin infects everything, including our thinking. Remember also that while the OIA *process* is an excellent tool, and one that Jesus models for us throughout the gospels, no process can grant the kind of divine illumination that God wants to provide as we study the Bible. [a]

Bible study ultimately becomes fruitful only when we approach the Bible rightly, in reliance on the Holy Spirit to grant us a measure of access to the very mind of Christ (1 Corinthians 2:6–16). What a joy, then, to know that if you want such access, all you have to do is ask (Luke 11:13).

---

a. Yes, God is fully able to break into our daily existence and reveal himself to us under any circumstances. But the consistent message of Scripture is that these are unusual events, and that it is primarily through his revealed Word that God chooses to communicate with us.

Two

From Familiarity to Observation

Five Elements and Four Skills

Valerie loved Jesus and served faithfully in church. But during Bible study, she was jumpier than a ticklish Leprechaun.

"This reminds me of something I read yesterday…"

"Charles Spurgeon said…"

"It's like the time when I…"

"How should I respond to people who say…?"

"Where did evil come from?"

"Where is the verse that says…?"

"After all, you know, when two or three are gathered together…"

The only way forward was to focus her. One simple question usually worked: "So how do you see that in the passage?"

Before we can set our eyes on the horizon, we have to get our noses in the text. Our study must begin with observation. When we observe, we try to figure out what the text says—not what we want it to say, think it should say, or heard someone else say about it. We receive each text on its own terms, and that process requires careful observation.

The Greatest Enemy of Observation is Familiarity

When I think I know something as well as I need to, I stop trying to learn more about it. This is just human nature, and much of the time it's a rational approach. How many stairs are in your house? What is the license plate number on your car? (If you have a vanity plate, your answer doesn't count.) If you don't know exactly, it probably doesn't matter too much. You are already as familiar with these things as you need to be. But when it comes to Scripture, we make a serious mistake when we allow familiarity to stop us from seeking to know more, or to know more clearly. In fact, when it comes to the Bible, familiarity can quickly become our enemy.

Much of the problem comes from the fact that what passes for familiarity is quite often simply wrong. Do you remember the story where the resurrected Jesus walks through a wall? It's in John 20:19 and 26, but read it again, observing carefully.

John says the doors were locked. He says Jesus came and stood among the disciples. But *he does not say Jesus walked through the wall.* In fact, because

John doesn't specify how Jesus got from outside the room to inside, there are lots of options. Maybe Jesus *did* walk through the wall, but perhaps he opened the door even though it was locked (easy for the one who did all those miracles). Maybe he stood at the door and knocked, and they heard his voice and let him in. Maybe he opened a hole in the roof and had some friends lower him on a pallet. I'm not trying to be irreverent; my point is that if we observe the text carefully, we cannot say how Jesus got into the room. Don't let familiarity with a passage stop you from observing the text—no matter how many times someone talks about "the time Jesus walked through a wall."

Your Turn
1. Pick your favorite Bible story. Read it five times in one sitting, using a different translation than usual. Find five new observations.
2. Study John 3:16 and see how many observations you can make.

The Book Overview Process

I have a child who spontaneously asks, "Hey Papa, do you remember that thing? You know, that thing?" When I ask for a little more information on "that thing," the child gets frustrated. Unfortunately, though, I can't answer the question until I get some context.

Similarly, if we isolate a verse from a passage, a passage from a chapter, or a chapter from its book, we're likely to skew our observations. Thus, we must first observe the whole book in which we find the section that interests us. This step is called "the book overview." We could address many issues during the book overview, but I find these four overview topics most helpful.

1. *Author*: Who wrote the book?

2. *Audience* and *Occasion*: To whom did the author write? What was going on in the lives of the author and the audience at the time?

3. *Themes* and *Structure*: What are the big ideas or episodes, and how are they arranged?

4. *Purpose*: Why did this author write these things to this audience at this time?

The best way to answer these questions is simply to read the whole book five or six times. That might seem scary and time-consuming, but you'll never learn to swim until you let go of the side of the pool.

Author, Audience, Occasion. Besides reading the book in question repeatedly, you can often get more background on these areas by searching the Bible for the names of key people and places connected to the book you want to study. For example, when you study First or Second Thessalonians, you can read passages in Acts that mention Thessalonica. You can learn about Old Testament prophets from the narrative books (2 Kings 14:23–27 will acquaint you with the prophet Jonah, for example)—just be aware that different characters might have the same name (like Joseph, Saul, Darius, or Abimelech).

Themes and Structure. Mapping out the larger structure of a book of the Bible can be challenging for detail-oriented thinkers, but you can start by tracing themes and noticing major changes in topic, characters, or setting. For more help, see a resource like David Dorsey's *The Literary Structure of the Old Testament.*[4]

Purpose. Once we know the author, audience, occasion, themes, and structure, we can find the book's purpose by taking the themes and asking (as I noted above) why this author wrote *these things in this way to these people at this time.* If the purpose still isn't apparent, help is available from additional resources, such as the book's introduction in a good study Bible.

Sometimes there are also details outside of the text that will help address the four general overview topics, so you may want to read a good overview article or entry in a Bible dictionary. Just make sure that whatever resource you consult gives the greatest weight to evidence from within the Bible itself. For example, many commentaries teach wrongly that one person wrote Isaiah 1–39, but a second person wrote Isaiah 40–66. However, the Gospel of John states clearly that the prophet Isaiah wrote both the first part (see John 12:39–40) and the second part (see John 12:38). A good scholar will trust such evidence from God's Word.

Sometimes you won't be able to come up with clear answers to one or more of the four overview topics. For example:

- We don't know the *author* of the book of Judges.
- There's some debate over the precise *audience* for Galatians.
- There's usually more than one good way to outline a book's *structure*.
- John leaves no doubt about the *purpose* of his Gospel (John 20:31), first letter (1 John 5:13), and third letter (3 John 9–10), but with the second letter we can only infer a purpose.

Nevertheless, if we go as far as we reliably can on these questions, we'll always be able to place the work within a reasonable historical context.

Genesis 1:1–2:3

Throughout this book, I'll use Genesis 1:1–2:3 to illustrate the steps of OIA, so let's begin with an overview of Genesis.

Author

Although Christians commonly teach that Moses wrote Genesis, the Bible doesn't explicitly attribute the book—or any quotes from it—to him. However, since biblical authors regularly treat the first five books of the Bible as "the Book of the Law of Moses" (Joshua 23:6; Nehemiah 8:1), we are justified in doing the same. Whether Moses penned the actual words of Genesis or not, he certainly saw fit to include the book in his collection of laws for Israel.

Audience and Occasion

Since Genesis doesn't come out and tell us who its intended audience is, we'll consult the *ESV Study Bible* for help: "It is reasonable to consider the first audience of the Pentateuch [Genesis through Deuteronomy] to be Israel in the wilderness (either the generation that left Egypt or their children)."[5] These people had just come out of slavery and were about to enter the land of promise, thus becoming a sovereign nation.

Themes and Structure

Genesis 1:1–2:3 opens the book by introducing God, his creative power, and his gracious delegation of authority to humanity. The book then proceeds in two main sections: early history (Genesis 2–11) and the history of Israel's forefathers (Genesis 12–50). These two main sections yield two main themes: God's work of creation and his promises to Abraham. Furthermore, the book is structured by ten "These are the generations" statements (Genesis 2:4, 5:1, 6:9, 10:1, 11:10, 27; 25:12, 19; 36:1; 37:2), which outline cycles of creation-fall-redemption-new creation. As humanity repeatedly fails to submit to God's gracious rule, God begins again with new generations.

Purpose

Why would Moses provide these people with this book at this time in their history? Well, consider everything they learned through this book that they may not have known previously. Through Genesis, the Israelites came to learn the beginning of the greatest and most important story ever, and they learned that God had placed them—above all peoples—at the center of that story. Imagine what an incredible message this was as they prepared to enter the Promised Land! Imagine the encouragement and sense of purpose it provided. Putting it all together, we can conclude that God gave the book of Genesis to the Israelites to establish a unifying national identity and a shared mission.

When my child asks if I remember "that thing," I ask questions that will help me establish a context. What thing? When did you see it? Where can I find it? Who was with you? Likewise, we can clarify a text's historical context with a book overview.

Your Turn

1. Read a helpful overview of Genesis (such as the one at bible.org/seriespage/1-introduction-genesis).
2. How will this historical context assist your study of each section?

Five Elements to Observe in a Passage

In 1997, pro golfer Tiger Woods won the Masters by twelve strokes and then did the unthinkable: he overhauled his swing. In 2002, after winning seven out of eleven Majors tournaments, he did it again. Why would he fix what wasn't broken? His own words: "Well, I thought I could become better. I've always taken risks to try to become a better golfer, and that's one of the things that has gotten me this far."[6] Each time, he went back to basics and drilled mechanics until they became instinctive and masterful.

Similarly, great Bible study begins with a few basic mechanics. Will you take the risk of learning them to become a better student of the Word? Whether you're an untested rookie or a seasoned professional, you can always improve at observing these five elements.

1. **Literary Form.** Is this passage a letter or a narrative? A prophecy, a collection of wisdom, or a song? What tools should I access on account of the literary form?

2. **Words.** Count how many times key words are repeated. Notice how various things are described or labeled. Keep track of how the narrator names the characters through the passage, and whether he changes their names or titles along the way.

3. **Grammar.** Identify the subject, verb, and object of each sentence. What are the main verbs? (This isn't as scary as it sounds; you're just looking for the actors and their actions.) In other words: who does what, and to whom or what is it done?

4. **Structure.** How does the passage fit together? Using tools corresponding to the literary form, break the text into paragraphs or stanzas. Notice transitions.

5. **Mood.** What tone does the author use? Does the passage inspire action, evoke emotion, or challenge assumptions?

Your Turn

1. Read Genesis 1:1–2:3 and begin to observe it.
2. What have you read before but didn't notice? How could these new observations affect your understanding of the passage?

Now let's take a look at each of these five elements in greater depth.

Observe Literary Form

Few things will influence your approach to a text more than literary form. Fee and Stuart's bestselling book on Bible interpretation focuses there, so I begin there.

> We affirm that there is a real difference between a psalm, on the one hand, and an epistle on the other. Our concern is to help the reader to read and study the psalms as poems, and the epistles as letters… These differences are vital and should affect both the way one reads them and how one is to understand their message for today.[7]

Literary form has to do with the style and set of conventions with which an author decides to communicate his message. If you pick up a piece of writing that begins, "Roses are red and violets are blue," you would immediately presume a few things about *how* to read that text. If it begins instead with "Dear Sir or Madam," your presumptions would be altogether different. And so on, if the document begins with "Once upon a time," or even "lol :-) <3."

There are two lenses through which we can view the element of literary form: genre and text type. *Genre* has much to do with the purpose and use of a text, while *text type* is primarily about the style or mode of writing. This may sound confusing at first, but it will make more sense after I explain each of these lenses. I'll begin with genre, as that lens is more frequently addressed in commentaries and books about Bible study.

Genre. A passage's genre is related to the purpose for which the author wishes his audience to use it. Is this text a historical account, meant to tell a story about what happened? Is it a letter, meant to be read publicly or instruct a community? Is it a song to be sung? Is it a law code to be obeyed? Is it a genealogy meant to trace an inheritance or lines of descent? Is it a gospel to narrate the life and mission of Jesus Christ?

There are many genres found in the Bible. In fact, English professor Leland Ryken has identified almost 300 "literary forms" present in the Bible, and he claims that over half of them could be labeled as genres.[8] But the most prevalent genres are historical narrative, law, wisdom literature, prophetic literature, gospel, letter, and apocalyptic literature. Less prevalent genres include lament psalm, song, proverb, parable, and genealogy.

Each genre needs to be read and understood on its own terms. For example, Luke wrote his gospel and the book of Acts as historical accounts of actual events, but in the book of Revelation, John communicates symbolically. Both books have similar trappings— telling a story—but because the genres are different, they must be read and understood differently. If you try to read Luke as symbolism, for example, you will be well on your way to joining the National Heresy Society. Books of the Bible must be read according to their genre.

Since I can't cover all the ramifications of genre in this short book, I commend Fee and Stuart's *How to Read the Bible for All Its Worth* for further study. I can, however, illustrate how to observe genre with, once again, Genesis 1:1–2:3 (which I'll call "Genesis 1" from now on).

Although genre is usually simple to identify, this passage happens to be a notable exception. Debates rage over Genesis 1 because most interpretations of the book derive from which genre people think it falls into.

- If Genesis 1 is a grand myth, it speaks more of what the ancients believed than what we should believe.

- If it's historical narrative, we hit some hard

> questions about compatibility with scientific theories.

- If it's poetic theology, it doesn't address history or science, so such questions are irrelevant.

My purpose is not to evaluate every proposal for the genre of Genesis 1,[9] but I will make a few observations of the text. The author reports events, telling a story through the use of characters, setting, plot, climax, and resolution.[b] He doesn't tell us he's narrating a parable (as Jesus often did, such as when he said, "The kingdom of heaven is like a merchant in search of fine pearls…"). Instead, he writes with a straightforward, matter-of-fact style: "God said… God created… It was so." This approach continues unchanged through the rest of Genesis, which is clearly historical narrative. I conclude, therefore, that Genesis 1 presents itself as historical narrative, just like the rest of Genesis.

The principal implication of this conclusion is that Genesis is about things that actually happened. Though Genesis 1 speaks of seemingly implausible things like creation from nothing, a good-but-initially-unfinished earth (v 2), and an eternal, almighty God whose words held it together (vv 1, 3, 6, etc.), the author presents none of it as fable or fairy tale. The author believed the creation to have taken place in a way that fits the

---

b. I will cover the use of tools such as characters, setting, plot, climax, and resolution later, when I explain the impact of *text type* on a text's *structure*.

written account. So did Moses (Exodus 20:11), Isaiah (Isaiah 42:5; 45:18), Jonah (Jonah 1:9), Nehemiah (Nehemiah 9:6), Paul (2 Corinthians 4:6), Peter (2 Peter 3:5), and Jesus (Mark 10:6). Those of us who believe in the essential factuality of Genesis 1 are in good company.

Your Turn

1. Why does genre matter? What might be the consequences of reading one genre as though it were another genre?
2. Practice observing genre with Genesis 2:4–25. What genre is the chapter presented as? How does this affect the way you will approach it?

A funny thing about historical narratives in Scripture. While we are on the subject of historical narratives, I need to clarify something that can easily trip up students of the Bible. This can be a tricky concept for us to grasp today, but scholars know without a doubt that throughout the ancient world, authors were often more concerned with communicating a point than with presenting a precise timeline of events.

For example, the four Gospels tell many of the same events in a different order from one another, and in Genesis numerous timelines are technically out of order. The writers of Scripture organize their narratives intentionally—whether or not they're chronological—to present things in a way that is both artful and memorable (a huge help during those millennia when books were rare and precious things).

- Joseph's tale is beautifully structured around pairs of dreams (Genesis 37–50).

- Exodus 7–10 artfully patterns the plagues against Egypt into three groups of three plagues.

- Matthew 8–9 presents three sets of three miracles of Jesus, with instruction on discipleship between the sets.

When you and I read Scripture and are confronted with a de-emphasis of literal timelines, we can get confused. We are tempted to think, *But wait, is that really how it happened?* Yet the biblical writers—along with a great many other ancient authors—would probably tell us, "Stop obsessing about that. What's truly central is not so much the *order* in which things happened, but the *significance* of what happened." They do have a point.

No need to worry, then. Order, art, and intention don't have to be opposed to history. The biblical writers, inspired by the Holy Spirit, often rearrange the order of various events—not because they "got their facts wrong," but intentionally, to make sure you and I get God's point! Because that's ultimately more important than what happened first, second, third, fourth, and on and on.

Text type.[10] A passage's text type has to do with the style of the writing itself. The text type is not another kind of genre but is an alternate and complementary lens through which to view the passage's literary form. Therefore, all genres can be written in any or all of the

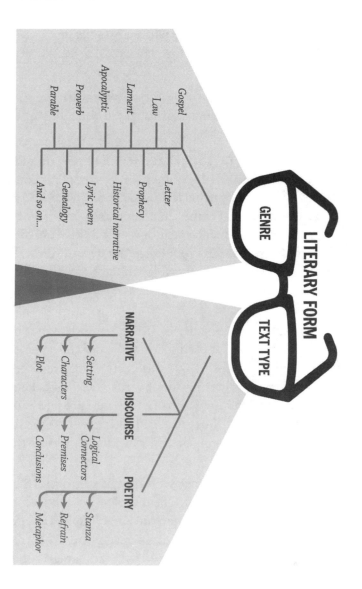

three text types. In fact, a single passage can alternate rapidly among the text types.

The three text types in the Bible are narrative, poetry, and discourse. Narrative is the text type of all prose stories, regardless of whether they are non-fiction (historical account) or fiction (parable or fable). Poetry is the primary text type for most of the wisdom and prophetic books, and we recognize biblical poetry by its parallel lines typically typeset with lots of white space on the page. Discourse is the text type for any kind of prose speech, whether it be quoted dialogues, transcribed sermons, law codes, or apostolic letters.

Sometimes, the category of text type may be even more useful to observe than genre, strictly defined. That is partly because there are only three options to remember, and partly because each text type has specific rules that hold great value when it comes time to interpret the passage (I'll explain many of those rules in a bit when I explain how to observe structure). In addition, as I mentioned above, a single passage, regardless of its genre, can alternate among all three text types. For example, the overall text type of Genesis 1 is narrative, as it is a story told in prose. But within that narrative both discourse (any time God's speech is directly quoted) and poetry (Genesis 1:27) are embedded. Noticing those shifts in text type now will assist proper interpretation later.

Your Turn

1. What is the overall text type of Genesis 2?
2. Does this passage have either (or both) of the other text types embedded within it? If so, where?

Observe Words

Douglas Wilson wrote, "Words are the bricks with which you build. Buy the bricks before starting on the wall." [11] He directed this advice to writers, but I'll commandeer his point for the sake of readers. Observe the bricks, and you'll be more likely to understand the wall.

The books of the Bible were constructed from stories. These stories were built from episodes. Episodes arose by the gathering of paragraphs. Paragraphs disemboweled produce sentences. Sentences dissect into words. Words are our bricks. Observe them well.

Let's practice by observing some of the key words in Genesis 1.

- *God.* A word repeated frequently is *God.* In fact, God is nearly the only actor in the story. God created. God said. God saw. God separated. God called. God made. God set. God blessed. God finished. God rested. At one point, "the earth brought forth" (v 12). Six times, evening "was," and morning "was" (vv 5, 8, 13, 19, 23, and 31). But God did everything else directly.

- *Let.* Another repeated word is *let.* God speaks his wish — "let there be" — and it comes to pass.

- *Good.* Notice one more repetition: "God saw that it was good." Good, good, good, good, good, good — six times (vv 4, 10, 12, 18, 21, 25). Good every day except Monday; twice on Tuesday. Then he makes humans, and in sum says all his creation is *very* good (v 31). This change signals a climax near the end of the chapter.

Repeated words. These are some of the simplest but most fruitful observations, and I begin every study with them. Get a Bible that you're willing to write in. Highlight repeated words with the same color, or circle or underline them. Once you do, some key ideas might just leap off the page.

Connectors. These are words like *therefore, in those days*, or *in the same way* that connect sentences, paragraphs, or chapters. Connectors might signal purpose ("in order to," "so that") or causation ("because"). Notice the connections and try to figure out why they're there. In Genesis 1, each day begins with the connecting word *and*, which strings the week together. Genesis 2:1 begins with *thus*, which signals a conclusion. Genesis 2:3 uses the word *so*, which reinforces the conclusive feel of these final verses.

Names and titles. These kinds of words develop characterization. God is *God* in Genesis 1, but he's the *Lord God* (that is, *Yahweh God*) in Genesis 2. *God* is a title of power and authority, but *Yahweh* is a personal, intimate name. To highlight the payoff of this skill, I'll give another example. Genesis 21:8–21 says a lot about Ishmael without ever using his name. He's always "the son of Hagar the Egyptian" or "the son of the slave woman" or simply "the boy." If you weigh this in the overall context of the passage, you can see that the author wants us to think of Ishmael as subservient to Isaac, who is the son of promise.

Now re-read Genesis 1 from the beginning and observe how the author uses key words.

- The chapter takes place "in the beginning," which is obviously the opening for an account of some kind, a story.

- In verse 1, God creates the *heavens* and the *earth*. These two words show up often in the chapter, but they're used in different ways.

  > The word *earth* appears numerous times (vv 1, 2, 10, 11, 12, 17, 20, 22, 24, 25, 26, 28, 29, 30, and 2:1) with multiple possible meanings. It clearly refers to the "dry land" in 10, 11, 12, etc., but in verse 26, "all the earth" seems to refer to the whole world that's been made: sea, air, and land.

  > The word *heavens* is also repeated (vv 1, 8, 14, 15, 17, 20, 26, 28, 30, and 2:1). It usually refers to the "expanse" (sky), fashioned and named on day two. I'm not sure whether *heavens* in 1:1 refers to this sky or to the highest heavens (the place we normally think of as heaven, where

God and the angels dwell). Either way, *heavens* in 2:1 clearly refers to the same heavens as 1:1.

- So both the heavens and the earth are created in 1:1, and by 2:1–2 both are complete. However, the intervening narrative focuses on the earth. Verse 2 speaks about only the earth and not the heavens, and this earth is incomplete: it is without *form*, it is *void* (empty), and *darkness* is over its face. But the Spirit of God is hovering, and the rest of the story tells of how God completes the earth.

I'm not saying that these "bricks" magically assemble themselves into a "wall" as soon as you identify them. At this point, they are just a pile of bricks. But they *are* something with which you can begin to build—and you can't build without them.

Your Turn

Practice observing words in Genesis 2:4–25. Write down repeated words, connectors, names or titles, and key terms.

Observe Grammar

The philosopher Ludwig Wittgenstein wrote, "Like everything metaphysical, the harmony between thought and reality is to be found in the grammar of the language."[12] My high school English teacher would say he was on to something.

Without grammar, we'd have trouble communicating. Consider what we'd lose if we gave up just one part of speech: verbs. We couldn't *do* or *be* anything. We'd have no predicates. Just subjects. All the time. No action. Maybe objects. Short sentences, though. Loads of confusion. Mass hysteria. Need for clarity. Not much *to say*. Aw, shoot; I couldn't do it.

Once you've observed the key words of a Bible text, observe how the author compiled those words into sentences. In other words, observe the grammar.

Grammar can be a scary word, invoking memories of pimples, bullies, and parental pressure from days gone by. But I'm here to tell you that grammar can be fun and exciting—as a gateway into fruitful observation of the Bible.

In the previous section on words, I dipped my toes into the grammar of Genesis 1. Now I'll wade in a bit more. Watch what happens if I strip every sentence down to just the subject and main verb.

- God created.
- The earth was, and darkness was.
- The Spirit was hovering.
- God said, "Let there be," and there was.
- God saw.
- God separated.
- God called.
- There was.

- God said, "Let there be."
- God made and separated.
- It was.
- God called.
- There was.

That takes us through verse 8. If you keep going, maybe using a particular highlighter color for the subjects and main verbs, you'll sketch the story's skeleton. You'll notice that, although God calls on the creation to participate in the work (for example, "let the waters swarm" in verse 20), the narrator almost always attributes the final action to God himself ("So *God created* the great sea creatures..." in verse 21).

My point here is simple: strip away the detail to observe the basic sentence structure, and we can observe the essential action. Remember, before we can see what the text means, we must observe what it says. One way to identify what the text says is to observe the grammar.

Your Turn

Practice observing grammar in Genesis 2:4–25. Strip sentences down to subjects and main verbs to see the flow of action.

Observe Structure

Geddy Lee of the band Rush once said, "That is what intrigues me; songwriting and song structure and expression." [13] As a music theorist, I share his interest in structure.

Much music is based on an A–B–A structure. You start with a musical idea, develop that idea (or go to a second idea), and then return home. "Twinkle Twinkle, Little Star" is a good example:

A: Twinkle twinkle, little star. How I wonder what you are.
B: Up above the world so high like a diamond in the sky.
A: Twinkle twinkle, little star. How I wonder what you are.

Like songwriters, authors communicate their ideas through intentional structure. Without clear structure, readers feel awash in a sea of details. And ancient authors in largely illiterate cultures couldn't rely exclusively on the printed word. They had to make use of patterning and repetition that would be noticeable when read aloud. Therefore, the message they sought to communicate was inextricably tied to the structural patterns with which they chose to communicate it. Consequently, the structure of a text is one of the most important observations we can make.

The structure of Genesis 1 has a distinct rhythm to it that's not difficult to perceive. Through this rhythm, the narrator shapes his ideas into a chronicle of seven days.

Units of thought. When observing the structure, our first goal should be to break the text up into major sections, identified by the author's *units of thought*.

Authors use a variety of literary devices to mark their units of thought for us. Repeated words or phrases, changes in setting, logical conclusions, and explicit verbal transitions could all serve as markers, depending on the genre and text type.

In Genesis 1, each "day" serves as a unit of thought within the chronicle. The rhythm and repetitions identify each unit, from the beginning "And God said" to the concluding "And there was evening and there was morning, the [Xth] day." And once we've observed those units of thought, it becomes clear that 1:1–2 and 2:1–3 stand outside the pattern. So the passage's basic structure has an introduction (1:1–2), six days of work (1:3–31), and a concluding day of rest (2:1–3).

Comparisons and contrasts. Sometimes the structure eludes us until we recognize *comparisons* and *contrasts*, which are connections that show how two or more things are similar (comparison) or different (contrast). Authors use these connections to package their ideas.

Some comparisons and contrasts occur on a small scale, within a single sentence, such as "the heavens and the earth" (a comparison in Genesis 1:1, where both realms were created in the beginning). But other comparisons and contrasts occur on a broader scale and may help with identifying units of thought. For example, the similarly narrated opening and closing of each of the first six days of creation help us to recognize each of those days as a unit of thought. We can then explore what makes each of those days *different* (contrasts) to discern how those units are related to one another—which I'll do in a bit when I unpack the rising action in Genesis 1. But first I must explain the impact of text type on our observation of structure.

Your Turn

Try to identify the units of thought in Genesis 2:4–25. Hint: Genesis 1 patterns the narrative by time ("days"), but Genesis 2 uses a different structural device.

Text type and structure. Earlier, we observed the literary form, in part, through the lens of text type. In light of those observations, we can now employ particular tools to help us observe the structure, as each text type tends to use different mechanisms for marking the structure of a passage. These mechanisms function like paint blazes on a wilderness trail to show us the contours of the author's message.

Discourses typically mark their structure by means of logical argumentation. In particular, discourses attempt to persuade readers of one or more *conclusions*, supported by evidence or a sequence of *premises*. So pay careful attention to transitional words and phrases, which can mark shifts in conclusion or content. Units of thought are typically marked by a primary conclusion; moving from one conclusion to the next signals a new paragraph. For example, the structure of Ephesians 2:1–10 can be outlined according to the following logical transitions:

1. "And you were" (vv 1–3)—describing the former state of affairs.

2. "But God" (vv 4–6)—describing how God interrupted that state of affairs.

3. "So that" (v 7)—revealing God's intentions for interrupting.

4. "For" (vv 8–9)—we need to investigate whether these verses summarize the overall conclusion, offer another reason for God's action, demonstrate evidence of his work, or do something else.

5. "For" (v 10)—we need to investigate whether this verse takes an additional step in the argument, or whether it is parallel to the previous "for" segment.

Poetry typically marks its structure by means of shifts in *metaphor*, shifts in *subject* or *object* (including shifts in *pronouns*), or *refrains*—a line or phrase repeated at regular intervals. Because poetry is highly emotional and evocative, the more sensitive we can be to these shifts, the better we'll be able to follow the poem's train of thought. Units of thought are typically marked by the prevailing metaphor or idea; moving from one overarching image to the next signals a new stanza. For example, the structure of Psalm 80 can be outlined according to these refrains and shifts in metaphor:

1. Metaphor of an attentive shepherd (vv 1–3)

> concluding refrain: "Restore us, O God; let your face shine, that we may be saved!"

2. Metaphor of an angry provider (vv 4–7)
> concluding refrain: "Restore us, O God of hosts; let your face shine, that we may be saved!"

3. Metaphor of a ravaged vine (vv 8–19)
> concluding refrain: "Restore us, O Lord God of hosts! Let your face shine, that we may be saved!"

Narrative typically marks its structure by means of its *plot*. This includes *characters* (who execute the plot) and *setting* (which hosts the plot), but is centered on conflict, rising action, climax, and resolution. Most narratives begin with a preliminary state of affairs (the setting). Then enters a conflict between characters to threaten that state of affairs. The rising action intensifies the conflict, up to the point of climax, where the conflict is fixed or reversed in some way. Then matters settle into a new state of affairs (a new setting).

Units of thought are typically employed in service of one complete plot arc; moving from one plot arc (or setting) to the next signals a new scene. For example, the structure of the days of Genesis 1 follows a simple plot arc:

1. Setting: God created heavens and earth (1:1)

2. Conflict: The earth has three problems: formlessness, emptiness, and darkness (1:2)

3. Rising action: God works on each of the three problems (1:3–31)

4. Climax: The heavens *and* the earth are finally finished (2:1)

5. Resolution into new setting: God rests and blesses the seventh day (2:2–3)

Unpacking the rising action in Genesis 1. When we observe the narrative text type of Genesis 1, we should figure out where the main source of tension, or conflict, is introduced. Verse 1 provides the setting for the entire chapter—in fact for the entire Bible—and verse 2 is where the tension begins. We're told that the earth was incomplete in three major ways: it was formless (lacking shape), empty (lacking stuff), and dark (lacking light). The subsequent verses describe how God addresses this narrative tension by bringing shape, stuff, and light into the creation.

- **Day One** (vv 3–5): creating light.

- **Day Two** (vv 6–8): shaping an "expanse" between waters above and below.

- **Day Three** (vv 9–13): shaping dry land and causing the earth to sprout vegetation.

- **Day Four** (vv 14–19): setting two great lights in the "expanse."

- **Day Five** (vv 20–23): making the waters swarm with fish, and letting birds multiply across the "expanse."

- **Day Six** (vv 24–31): making the earth bring forth living creatures, and making man in God's image.

- **Day Seven** (2:1–3): resting because the work is finished.

Notice how days one through six show God (present by his Spirit) correcting the earth's three flaws from verse 2. Notice also the structure, in this case A–B–B–A–C–C.

A: **Day One** addresses the *darkness*.

B: **Day Two** addresses the *formlessness*.

B: **Day Three** addresses the *formlessness*, then the *emptiness*.

A: **Day Four** addresses the *darkness*.

C: **Day Five** addresses the *emptiness*.

C: **Day Six** addresses the *emptiness*.

When day seven (Genesis 2:1–3) describes God as having "finished his work," it highlights the completeness of the structure. Though God creates the heavens and an incomplete earth in the beginning, he completes his work over the course of six days. Then he rests from his creative work on the heavens and the earth.

The beautiful plot structure raises a few questions. *Why did God do it this way? Why not just make it all to perfection in the first instant?* But these questions lead us into interpretation, so let's hang on to them until we get to that part of the OIA process. The structure may be one of the most challenging and time-consuming categories to observe. But it bears fruit thirty-, sixty-, and a hundred-fold when it comes time to interpret the author's meaning.

Your Turn

1. In light of the overall text type of Genesis 2:4–25, what will be your chief tools to observe the structure?
2. Use those tools now to discern the detailed structure of Genesis 2:4–25

Observe Mood

The Scottish writer Thomas Carlyle said, "There are good and bad times, but our mood changes more often than our fortune." [14] Just like us, the mood of those whom God used to write Scripture changed often. Because mood deals more with feeling than thought, it is more slippery than genre, words, grammar, or structure. Nevertheless, mood still provides a major clue to the author's intentions.

What is mood? Let me illustrate the idea with a few statements.

1. I'm not upset with you.

2. I'm *not* upset with you.

3. I'm not upset with *you*.

4. I'M NOT UPSET WITH YOU!!!

Can you sense a different intention behind each of those statements? While it's true that biblical literature didn't have conventions like bold text, italics, or exclamation points, the ancients were no strangers to communicating mood.

Read Genesis 1 out loud. What sort of mood do you sense?

- "In the beginning" prepares you for something weighty and profound.

- "The earth was without form and void" presents a staggering problem.

- "The Spirit of God was hovering over the face of the waters" moves you with a sense of mystery and anticipation.

- "And God said… And it was so." Repeatedly, God shines and separates. He shapes and populates. Order reigns, and chaos subsides.

- "Let us make man in our image, after our likeness." The drama builds to this peak: God replicates himself on the earth (in a manner of speaking). He delegates dominion to his human subjects. Though God rests from his work (Genesis 2:1–3), his labors—illuminating the darkness, shaping the formlessness, and filling the emptiness—continue as men and women multiply and subdue (1:28).

As you read the opening chapters of Genesis, the mood soars. Observe it, and you can't help being moved.

Your Turn

1. In Genesis 2:4–25, how does the mood change?
2. How does it stay the same?

Four Key Observation Skills

Now that I've walked through the five elements for observation, I'll highlight four simple tips. I usually begin my study with these because they're not too difficult and they pay well. If you ever get stuck (or don't know how to start), try these four skills. I list each one with its category so you can go back to that section of this chapter and locate further explanation of the skill.

1. Observe Words: specifically, *repeated words*

2. Observe Words: specifically, *connectors*

3. Observe Words: specifically, *names and titles*

4. Observe Structure: specifically, *comparison and contrast*

These tips give you four hooks on which to hang your observations, and the following Observation Worksheet offers a helpful way of organizing what you have discovered. In this way, you can anchor your study in the text and prepare yourself for interpretation, the subject of our next chapter.

Your Turn

1. Practice these four observation skills with Genesis 2:4–25.
2. Study John 3:16 again and use your new skills to make 50 observations.
3. You may photocopy the following worksheet (or download a larger version from www.knowableword.com/resources) to help with observation.

OBSERVATION WORKSHEET

Text: _____

Introductory Observation

List the repeated words.	What names or titles do characters have?
What things are compared or contrasted?	List connectors and how they're used.

Detailed Observation

Literary Form:

Words:

Grammar:

Structure:

Mood:

Three

From Presumption to Interpretation

Keys to Understanding

Few things are sweeter than seeing someone get it.

I'm studying Ephesians 1 with two guys—a young Christian and his unbelieving roommate—when the roommate suddenly exclaims, "The Ephesians never would have gotten all those good things from God if Jesus hadn't died! It's only through his blood that they have adoption, forgiveness, and an inheritance."

He nails the text's meaning, and his fresh insight sets me up to ask the next question: "So do you think it would be worth it to hope in Christ?"

In the Observation phase, we discover *what* a passage says. In the Interpretation phase, we uncover *why* the passage says it. When we understand the "why," we've identified the text's meaning, and then we're ready to get practical (the Application phase). This chapter will teach you how to find the "why."

Why We Interpret

I remember the moment when one of my daughters entered the interpretation phase of life. It happened when she was only two. We got home from church, and my wife told the children to get out of the van and go into the house. My darling little girl immediately asked, "Why?"

We interpret because God made us to interpret. Communication always moves beyond the "what" to the "why." We interpret grunts as displeasure and lingering glances as seeds of romance. Averted eyes indicate uncertainty or deceit. Such analysis is a universal part of life. Communication always moves from observation to interpretation.

Therefore, you should make the move in Bible study as well. Don't stop with observation, but continue forward to understand the "why." If you don't interpret well, you may miss the point of the text. And since the point is to know God through his Son Jesus and receive eternal life, I presume you won't want to miss it.

Your Turn

Look over your notes from Genesis 1. As you consider your observations, what "why" questions come to mind?

The Greatest Enemy of Interpretation is Presumption

Presumption—the fruit of familiarity—is the act of drawing conclusions from limited evidence. Courts presume defendants to be innocent (a good thing!) until the body of evidence convicts beyond all doubt. When you drive through a green light, you presume the opposing traffic sees a red light. Furthermore, you presume those drivers won't hit the gas until they see green.

Since you're not omniscient, every decision you make is based on some degree of presumption. So while the word itself often gets a bad rap, there's nothing inherently wrong with presumption, and avoiding it completely is impossible.

At the same time, however, presumption is deadly when it trumps careful investigation. Unrestrained presumption can obstruct the process of interpretation.

Let's say you want to buy a house. You find one you like, and sign a contract to purchase it. You pack your things and prepare to relocate your family. But on move-in day, you find the "seller" didn't actually own the house. He's powerless to hand it over to you. In fact, another family is living in the house with no intention of moving. You're stuck, partly because you presumed too much.

Presumption can have devastating consequences for big life decisions, but it also causes trouble in the mundane. We presume that a curt reply indicates anger. We mistake friendliness for attraction. We impute motives. We scold and convict a child on the testimony of a single embittered sibling. We rush to our conclusions and find security in the strength of our convictions. We admit no further evidence.

Careless presumption will kill your Bible study. It will strangle observation and bear stillborn application. It will make you look like the stereotypical, narrow-minded Christian, and it will diminish your influence for the Lord. By strengthening your confidence in questionable conclusions, presumption will cloud your relationship with Jesus and your experience of his grace. When it comes to Bible study then, guard yourself against every form of unexamined presumption.

Forms of Presumption

Relativism—believing a text means whatever we want it to mean—can be a form of presumption. We're not compelled to investigate the evidence, so we're "tossed to and fro by the waves and carried about by every wind of doctrine, by human cunning, by craftiness in deceitful schemes" (Ephesians 4:14). We lose our anchor in Christ.

Tradition can be a form of presumption when it bullies observation, threatens investigation, and demands adherence to a sanctioned message. Now I'm no hater of tradition; it's both valuable and necessary. But when it drives—and isn't driven by—interpretation, it rampages and destroys like a toddler in a Lego city. Unexamined tradition trains people to think only what they were taught to think, which may or may not be the truth.

Education can be a form of presumption when, like tradition, it generates thoughts but not thinkers. Irresponsible education—whether theistic or atheistic—results in students who presume to know the Bible, but who have ceased listening to it. For such learners, Jedi Master Yoda may prove instructive: "You must unlearn what you have learned."

Premature application can be a form of presumption when we jump to conclusions in the name of relevance. We read and observe the text, but we move straight to application. We want our answers to be quick and practical, but we fail to base our applications on what the text is actually saying.

Authority can be a form of presumption when we carelessly trust what the experts say about a text. We might learn to regurgitate their conclusions, but we won't learn to reach them ourselves. Our teaching will lack substantiation, and the next generation will grow disillusioned by what it perceives to be hollow.

Tradition, education, application, and authority are all good things. In the right context, presumption is a good thing. But unchecked, it will stifle your ability to interpret Scripture.

Your Turn

1. How might presumption hinder your interpretation of Genesis 1 and 2?
2. What have you been taught about Genesis 1 and 2? How can you allow the text to speak louder than your tradition or education?

Three Steps for Interpreting the Bible

The OIA method can be diagrammed in the shape of a big X. To interpret, we assemble and investigate our many observations until we understand the text's meaning. Since we'll continue observing new things in God's Word until Jesus returns, our observations could be infinite in number. But interpretations are not infinite (though our grasp of them may mature over time). Biblical authors had agendas, and we are not authorized to add to those agendas. We investigate the facts of the text until we're able to think the author's thoughts after him. And since biblical authors wrote God's very words, good interpretation trains us to think God's thoughts. It's like when husbands and wives complete each other's sentences, only better.

Three steps will enable you to conduct a sound investigation.

Ask Questions of Your Observations

Take your observations and ask lots of questions about them. Tackle those observations from every direction. Be as inquisitive as possible. Get better at asking questions, and you'll get better at interpreting.

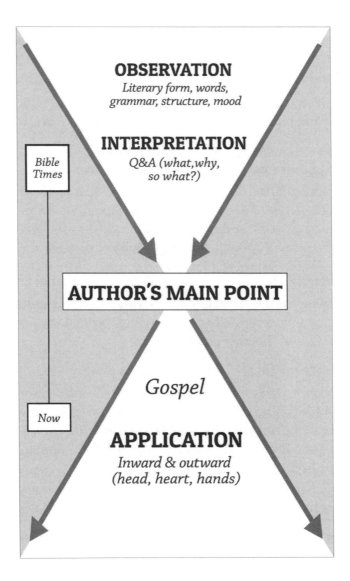

Your *questions* should be about your *observations* of the text. Don't ask every question that comes to mind, and don't feel the need to be clever. Your job is not to innovate, but to uncover. If your observation was poor, your interpretation won't be any better. (Note how the disciples didn't observe well, and so jumped to the wrong conclusion in John 21:22–23.)

Answer the Questions from the Text

Once you've asked your questions, answer them. There's one critical rule: answer questions only if they are answered—explicitly or implicitly—in the text (Proverbs 30:5–6). Don't chase rabbits through the trails of your mind. Don't use minor details to make the text say what you want it to say. Don't build a theology from one unclear verse. Instead, answer only those questions that are either assumed or addressed in the text. Let the rest go.

Determine the Author's Main Point

Your investigation should lead you to the main point of the passage. Sometimes the author's main point is explicit (for example, Hebrews 8:1), but many times it's not. Either way, uncovering the main point should be the goal of interpretation.

The main points of the Bible are the ones worth fighting for because they represent the main things God wants us to understand. We may draw conclusions about secondary or debatable points, but such conclusions must never drown out the Bible's main points in our thinking or teaching (Matthew 23:23–24).

With these three steps and a healthy dose of God's Holy Spirit, you're ready to interpret. The next few sections will elaborate on these three steps.

Your Turn

As you prepare for interpretation, remember that you need help from the Holy Spirit. Ask him now for insight into Genesis 1 and 2.

Ask Questions of Your Observations

Albert Einstein once said, "I have no special talent. I am only passionately curious." [15] I wish I were as talentless as he was! But though I'm no Einstein, I can still be like a scientist, fostering passionate curiosity. I can begin with observation and investigate with rigor.

The main questions are: *What?*, *Why?*, and *So what?* [16]

- **What** questions clarify or define your observations, e.g., "*What* does that phrase mean?" (*Who*, *Where*, *When*, and *How* questions do the same.) Such questions transition you from observation to interpretation.

- **Why** questions uncover the author's purpose, e.g., "Why did he say that?" These could be considered the essence of interpretation.

- **So what** questions draw out the implications,

as in, "So, what does he want us to do about it?" They transition you from interpretation to application.

Remember the five elements to observe from the previous chapter? Mesh these together with the three types of interpretive questions and we have a total of fifteen categories of interpretation to explore.

Interpretation Worksheet #1 may help you flex your investigative muscles. Don't feel compelled to fill in every block, but use the blocks to consider questions that might not be obvious to you. Over time, your study will become more organic and less structured than this worksheet may seem to suggest.

To interpret Genesis 1, we can ask these three types of questions for each of the five types of observations we made in the previous chapter.

The *What* Questions

Literary Form: *What* is the connection between this narrative and scientific theories of origins?

Words: *What* are the "heavens" in verse 1? Are they the same or different from "heaven" in verse 8? / *What* does it mean to be "without form" or "void"? / *What* is a "day" in Genesis 1? Is it the same thing we mean by "day"? / *What* is the difference between "livestock" and "beasts of the earth" in verse 24?

Grammar: *What* does it mean to be "made in God's image"?

INTERPRETATION WORKSHEET #1

-- -- -- -- -- Interpretive Questions -- -- -- -- -- -- -- --

	Observation	What?	Why?	So What?
Literary Form				
Words				
Grammar				
Structure				
Mood				

Structure: *When* were Satan and the angels created? / *How* did plants survive without pollinating insects?

Mood: *What* about Day Six makes the creation "very good"?

The *Why* Questions

Literary Form: *Why* does the author tell of earth's origin in the genre of historical narrative?

Words: *Why* is earth initially formless, empty, and dark?

Grammar: *Why* doesn't God make a finished earth in verse 1? / *Why* does God delegate dominion to humanity? / *Why* does God make both men and women in his image? / *Why* does God rest? Is he worn out?

Structure: *Why* does God take six days to finish the earth? / *Why* does God tackle earth's three areas of incompleteness one at a time?

Mood: *Why* does the chapter climax with Day Six?

The *So What* Questions

Literary Form: *So, what* effect will the narrative text type have on our reading of the text?

Words: *So, what* is our world like now? Does it still have any formlessness, shapelessness, or darkness?

Grammar: *So, what* does God expect of humanity as being made in his image? / *So, what* might get in the way of these expectations? / *So, what* might cause humanity to lose the image of God? Is that possible? / *So, what* does godly dominion look like in everyday life? / *So, what* did this dominion mandate mean for the original audience? / *So, what* does this mean for vegetarianism, environmentalism, animal rights, and ecology (or other issues we face today)?

Structure: *So, what* is our purpose in work and rest, and how does it mirror God's purpose?

Mood: *So, what* role do God's words on Day Six serve in the context of the whole chapter?

You may disagree with how I categorized some of these questions. That's okay. OIA isn't a hard science; it's a helpful set of tools. What matters is that you learn to use these tools to foster curious, honest, fruitful investigation.

Your Turn

Generate a list of questions from your observation of Genesis 2:4–25.

Answer the Questions from the Text

As I wrote above, answer only those questions *from* the text that are answered (explicitly or implicitly) *by* the text. That is, only those questions where the text *assumes* the original readers would know the answer, or the text *addresses* or provides the answer.

Answers assumed. Some answers are *assumed* in the text. The original audience would have known these answers, but we probably won't because of the millennia that separate our lives from theirs. Today we need reference material to help us understand what scholars have learned about ancient cultures. We can also check related Scripture passages to illuminate the text at hand. For example, the original readers of Genesis 15 would have understood what it meant to split an animal and pass between the pieces, but we need Jeremiah 34:18–20 to explain this ancient cultural practice.

In Genesis 1, some of our questions have answers that the text assumes.

- *What* are "the heavens" in verse 1? *Answer:* Israelites about to enter Canaan might know them as a place people aspired to reach (Genesis 11:4) but only God could possess (Deuteronomy 10:14).

- *What* does it mean to be "void"? *Answer: Strong's Exhaustive Concordance* defines it as "emptiness."

- *What's* the difference between "livestock" and "beasts of the earth" in verse 24? *Answer:* commentator Bruce Waltke sees it as a "contrast between domesticated and wild animals,"[17] although you might have figured that out just from the vocabulary.

- *So, what* about vegetarianism? Are we supposed to be vegetarians (v 29)? *Answer:*

investigation leads us to Genesis 9:3, which shows that God later allowed people to eat meat.

Most of these answers would have been obvious to someone who spoke Hebrew and lived during the time of Moses. But we in the twenty-first century often need outside help. Sometimes, as with the last question, we just have to keep reading and return to the question when a later passage addresses it further.

Answers addressed. Some answers are *addressed* in the text, either explicitly or implicitly. Answering these questions will often lead to new questions, compelling further investigation.

- *What* does it mean to be made in God's image? *Answer:* to be "after his likeness" (v 26). In other words, God made humans to be like him.

- Then, according to this passage, *what* does it mean to be like God? *Answer:* to do what God just did. To follow his pattern of addressing incompleteness by illuminating, shaping, and filling.

- Then, *what* should human dominion of the earth look like? *Answer:* illuminating, shaping, and filling the earth as God's ambassadors.

- *Why* does God take six days to finish the earth? *Answer:* to set a pattern for humanity to follow when he delegates dominion to them on Day Six.

- *So, what* does God expect humanity to do as his image-bearers? *Answer:* to illuminate, shape, and fill the earth.

- *What* does it mean to fill the earth? *Answer:* to be fruitful and multiply (v 28).

- *What* does it mean to shape the earth? *Answer:* to subdue the earth and rule over the various categories of creatures—fish of the sea, birds of the heavens, every living thing that moves on the earth (v 28).

- *What* does it mean to illuminate the earth? *Answer:* this answer is unclear and may be assumed in the text. Perhaps it means to relay God's instructions to all creation (vv 29–30).

- *Why* does God rest? *Answer:* with humanity in place to take dominion, his work of creating is finished.

Other kinds of questions. Finally, some of our questions are neither assumed nor addressed in the text. We should let them go until another passage addresses them for us.

- *What* is the connection between this narrative and scientific theories of origins?

- *When* were Satan and the angels created?

- *How* did plants survive without the pollinating role of insects?

- *Why* does God delegate dominion to humanity? (David asked this same question in Psalm 8.)

- *So, what* might cause humanity to lose the image of God? Is that possible?

Your Turn

1. What answers to your questions can you find in Genesis 2?
2. What questions should you let go?

Determine the Author's Main Point

I know… by the time you've gotten this far you're swirling in details. Five categories of observation and three types of interpretive questions produced fifteen options for investigation. And you've realized that you need to release a few of the questions that most interest you. You began this book thinking you'd dabble in the magic of Bible study, but the spell has taken over and the water line has exceeded flood stage. You're tempted to cue "The Sorcerer's Apprentice" and drown your exhaustion in a bucket of popcorn.

Don't lose hope. Everything we've done has a purpose, which is to help us know God better. We're almost there; we just need to pull it all together. My intention is not to impress people with long lists of questions and answers but to integrate those questions and answers into a coherent main point.

Such integration matters because ancient authors

didn't waste space with meaningless details. Every word has a purpose. Every sentence captures an idea. Every paragraph advances the agenda. And every section has a main point. The accumulation of these points promotes the goal of bringing the audience closer to the Lord. And once we understand how that main point directed the original audience toward the Lord, we'll be ready to consider how it should shape us.

Thus, for Genesis 1, the main point must be something more than "God created everything," or else the author could have stopped after verse 1. His intention led him to craft the narrative (and all its details) the way he did.

How Do We Find the Main Point?

The challenge of interpretation is to discover the "why" of the passage. Why is this text here? Why did the author write these things in this way?

Always Ask "Why?"

Often we spend so much time on the "what" that we forget to seek the "why," and we mistakenly believe we know the "why" because we've discovered the "what." For example, if we focus our study of Genesis 1 on figuring out which modern view of the days is the correct one, we'll inhibit comprehension. We might get the "what" (What is the length of each day?), but we won't necessarily get the "why" (Why does the author tell the story of creation as a sequence of seven days?). We must cultivate the discipline of asking why.

Though most Bibles have headings at the beginning of each section (Genesis 1 in ESV: "The Creation of the World"), these headings are usually observation summaries and not interpretive main points. These summaries may help when you're flipping through and trying to find a specific section, but they don't always capture the passage's main point. If you want to convert these summary headings to main points, sometimes you only have to ask *why*. For example, *why* does this passage tell of the creation of the world?

Since our observations and interpretive questions could be infinite in number, there are many pathways from the text's details to the main point. Most of these pathways are found by continually asking *why*. And if the main point is truly the main point, we should be able to carve a path from any detail in the passage to that main point.

Account for the Context

In the last chapter, we saw how the book overview places the work in history. This historical context influences our reading of the text and helps us to see the main point. In the case of Genesis 1, we see God shaping the nation of Israel, even as he shapes the whole earth. He's showing this nation how to be his people, made in his image, bringing his light, shape, and substance into the darkness, formlessness, and emptiness of their world.

In addition to the historical, two further types of context should guide us.

First, examine the literary context. What was the main point of the previous section of text? How does the author move from that section into this section? What issues lingered at the end of that section, and how does this section address those issues? Because Genesis 1 is the beginning, we have no prior literary context. Instead, this chapter will establish the context for everything that follows. Thus, we should read Genesis 2:4–25 (and following passages) in light of Genesis 1:1–2:3.

Second, examine any inter-textual context. That is, use a search engine or cross-references [18] to find other parts of the Bible that quote this section (or are quoted by it), and figure out the connections between them. When God inspired authors to quote other passages, he was showing us how to interpret those passages.

Though alluded to constantly, Genesis 1:1–2:3 is quoted explicitly only three times in the New Testament. In Mark 10:1–12, Jesus uses the creation account to set a pattern for human existence, particularly for marriage and divorce. In 2 Corinthians 4:1–6, Paul uses the creation account to justify his ministry of the gospel, which illuminates the darkness of people's hearts. In Hebrews 4:1–16, the author uses the creation account to motivate his audience to believe God's Word and so rest from their works just as God rested from his.

Track the Author's Flow of Thought

Ask: *how did the author get from the first verse to the last verse?* Here is where your observation of the structure will pay exceptional dividends. Since you've broken the passage up into sections, or units of thought, according to the literary markers utilized by the text type (which we discussed toward the end of the Observe Structure section in Chapter 2), your interpretive questions and answers should help you determine the main point of each section.

Then, string those points together to see how one unit of thought moves to the next. Once you've determined how the sections relate to one another, you can figure out which section bears the weight and force of the message. From there you can discern the main point of the entire passage.

For example, the main point of a **discourse** will have something to do with the *chief conclusion* being drawn from the sequence of evidence or premises. Other conclusions will be drawn along the way in support of the larger point being argued. But in order to grasp the author's main point, you'll need to clarify exactly which conclusion is the overall conclusion being argued for. In Ephesians 2:1–10, the argument goes as follows, with the main point being the chief conclusion of section three (v 7):

1. The natural state of affairs: "You were dead…" (vv 1–3)

2. God's interruption: "But God… made us alive… raised us up… and seated us" with Christ (vv 4–6)

3. God's intention: "So that he might show the riches of his grace to the ages" (v 7)

4. Summary of God's interruption: "You've been saved by grace and not your own doing, *so no one may boast*" (vv 8–9)

5. Summary of God's intention: "We are his workmanship," trophies of his grace (v 10)

The main point of a **poem** could be derived from a number of factors, depending on the poem. Perhaps the poem functions almost like a discourse, where one stanza states the *chief conclusion* and other stanzas parade forth evidence in service of that conclusion. Perhaps the poem asks a question whose answer comes at the middle or end of the poem—in which case that answer is likely to be the main point. Perhaps the poem illustrates many repetitions of a pattern, and that pattern is either the main point itself or a reflection of some other idea that is the main point. To illustrate with Psalm 80, the poem's three stanzas have a clear direction, where the second stanza contrasts with the first, leading to the dramatic and tender appeal of the third. That third stanza therefore bears the weight of the poem's argument, and we ought to focus our scrutiny there for the main point:

1. Attentive Shepherd: we know where to find the strength that saves (vv 1–3)

2. Angry Provider: but we're still being denied the strength that saves (vv 4–7)

3. Ravaged Vine: this isn't how it ought to be (vv 8–19)

The main point of a **narrative** will have something to do with the plot's *climax and resolution*. In order to grasp the author's main point, you'll need to clearly identify the point of climax and come to understand what exactly is being fixed or reversed by that climax. For Genesis 1, we began this process in the previous chapter when we observed the structure. We noted that:

- the prelude introduces the creation and the three areas of incompleteness (formlessness, emptiness, and darkness);

- Day One addresses the darkness;

- Day Two addresses the formlessness;

- Day Three addresses the formlessness and the emptiness;

- etc.

The passage climaxes *after* Day Six, when the heavens *and the earth* were finished — a state of affairs attained only after God delegates dominion to his human subjects. He creates them to be like him. This God, who labored to illuminate, shape, and fill, now calls men and women to do the same. They are to shine his light (possibly his word, truth, or glory), shape his world (subdue it and rule it), and fill it up with more people who will continue the work (be fruitful and multiply). As they labor, their heavenly Father will provide them with all the sustenance and instruction they need (vv 29–30).

So, having compiled all my observations and interpretations, I come up with this main point:

> *God's creative work sets a pattern for human dominion of the earth, and therefore humanity realizes its potential when it illuminates, shapes, and fills the earth in God's name.*

What did this mean for Israel in Moses' day? They would advance God's kingdom by believing and acting on God's promises to Abraham (Genesis 12:1–3). In other words, they would image God by subduing the land of promise (shaping), multiplying in it (filling), and making God's blessing available to all nations (illuminating).

What does this mean for us today? We, too, replicate God (in a sense) and fulfill our calling as God's people by illuminating, shaping, and filling the earth in God's name. But *how* do we do that? Our answer to this question must account for the context and begin with the mission of Jesus.

Your Turn

1. Why is it so challenging to figure out an author's main point?
2. Why is it critical that we do so?
3. According to the tools for the appropriate text type explained above, which part of Genesis 2:4–25 would you expect to bear the weight and force of the message?
4. What is the main point of Genesis 2:4–25?

Context Matters

In the steps above, I encouraged you to "account for the context" when interpreting the passage, and this important concept warrants further reflection. The skill of accounting for the context can't be acquired by memorizing a list of steps. It requires careful observation and clear thinking. So instead of merely telling you how to do it, I'll show you an extended example that involves all three kinds of context: historical, literary, and intertextual.

Perhaps you've heard Jesus' cry of dereliction while hanging on the cross: "My God, my God, why have you forsaken me?" (Mark 15:34). Perhaps you knew Jesus was alluding to David's lament in Psalm 22:1. But what exactly was David's concern, and why was it so devastating? And how did Jesus share that experience in his own crucifixion?

When we learn to find the main point by accounting for the context, we may find that some familiar phrases take on entirely new meanings.

David's Crisis of Faith

In Psalm 22, David feels utterly abandoned by God ("My God, my God, why have you forsaken me?"). The reason is that, as he looks around, he sees no evidence of God's presence or activity to save ("Why are you so far from saving me?"). David cries and cries but receives no answer (Psalm 22:1–2).

David understands how these things work, and he seeks to console himself with the perspective of history. In Israel's covenant with her God, there is a direct connection between loyal trust and deliverance.

- In you our fathers trusted (Psalm 22:4a).

- They trusted, and you delivered them (Psalm 22:4b).

- To you they cried and were rescued (Psalm 22:5a).

- In you they trusted and were not put to shame (Psalm 22:5b).

Those who trusted in God were rescued, and those who proved disloyal were put to open shame. This strengthens David to persevere in trust and believing loyalty (Psalm 22:3).

"But I am a worm and not a man" (Psalm 22:6). The problem is, it's not working as expected. David has trusted and remained loyal, but he is still put to shame! He is mocked and scorned. His trust in Yahweh is now the very thing for which he is mocked (Psalm 22:8).

The connection between trust and deliverance appears to be broken. For generations, the Israelites had a pattern of abandoning God when things didn't go their way. Will David do the same, especially now that he has seemingly hard evidence that trust in God will not pay off? Will he "go back to Egypt"? Will he grumble and complain? Will he turn to other gods?

In the rest of the psalm, we see David mature from a questioner (vv 1–10), to a beggar (vv 11–21), then to a preacher (vv 22–26), and finally to a missionary (vv 27–31). He withstands the test and survives the crisis of faith. With all outward appearances to the contrary, he proclaims that Yahweh remains worthy of fear (v 23), praise (v 25), and service (v 30).

Jesus' Crisis of Faith

Though David felt that God had abandoned him, we can confidently conclude that this was not truly the case (2 Samuel 7:9, 12–15). Yet for Jesus, such abandonment by the Father was in fact a reality. He faced his darkest hour alone (Mark 15:33–34), accompanied only by the sin of the world that had now become his own (2 Corinthians 5:21).

Once again, we must ask the question of historical habits: will Jesus survive the crisis of faith? Will he fall to pieces, just like generation upon generation of Jews had done before him? Since trust in the Father is not paying out in deliverance, is it worth it for him to continue trusting at all?

This tension is all the greater when we observe Mark's attention to the question of perseverance. Will Jesus see his commitment to crucifixion through until the end? Those who deride him dare him to come down from the cross (Mark 15:29–30). They doubt his ability to attain salvation for himself (v 31). They claim they will believe what he has said, only if he will come down (v 32). If he can't save himself, they wonder whether Elijah will come to take him down from the cross (v 36).

But Jesus perseveres. He stays on the cross until all is finished, and he can proclaim that "he has done it" (Psalm 22:31; see John 19:30). He remains loyal, even when abandoned by his Father. Because the Father despised and abhorred the affliction of the afflicted, and hid his face from him (Psalm 22:24), all the families of the nations can now worship before him (Psalm 22:27).

And though the answer was delayed three days, we know that he who cried out to his Father was eventually heard (Psalm 22:24, Romans 1:4, Hebrews 5:7–9).

Resist Your Familiarity and Account for the Context

"My God, my God, why have you forsaken me?" When you hear or recite the question, don't allow its familiarity to dull your senses to the visceral conflict it betrays. Delight in this hero, who succeeded in every way where Old Covenant Israel failed. Behold the crisis of faith, the disillusionment, and the unbelievable temptation to come down from the cross to prove his worth. And rest assured that you will never have to experience such complete abandonment, because he already went through it once for all.

Tell the coming generations of his righteousness, and that he has done it.

Context matters.

Your Turn

1. How does the context of Genesis 1 prepare you to study Genesis 2:4–25?
2. What questions linger from Chapter 1 that the reader of Genesis might expect to be addressed in Chapter 2?
3. How does the intertextual context (places where other parts of the Bible quote from Genesis 2) help you to understand what's happening in Genesis 2:4–25?

How to See Jesus in Any Bible Passage

In Chapter 1, we saw that the goal of Bible study is to know Jesus. Every passage of Scripture should take us to Jesus.

Now, in seminary I was told to be very careful here. Apparently, some ancient Christian interpreters thought they could see Jesus in every Old Testament breath, flower, and beast of the earth. So someone treated Rahab's scarlet cord (Joshua 2:18) as a prophecy of the flowing blood of Christ that would save her and her family. And someone else read the ten camels of Abraham's servant (Genesis 24:10) as symbols of the Ten Commandments, which would be fulfilled in

Christ. While some Old Testament passages directly predict the coming of the Hebrew Messiah (*Christ* in Greek), few hinge on such overt associations.

So if we shouldn't make arbitrary connections from the Old Testament to Jesus, what did Jesus mean when he said that all the Scriptures were about him? How can we make legitimate connections between shadow and reality (Hebrews 10:1)? Luke 24:46–47 provides a helpful template: "Thus it is written, that the Christ should *suffer* and on the third day *rise* from the dead, and that *repentance and forgiveness* of sins should be *proclaimed* in his name to all nations, beginning from Jerusalem."

Every passage of Scripture reveals Jesus by explaining at least one of the following truths about his work:[c]

Truth #1: The Messiah would suffer (die) and rise from the dead.

Truth #2: We must repent of our sins and be forgiven.

Truth #3: This message—that the Messiah's death and resurrection make forgiveness possible— must be proclaimed to all nations.

So rather than looking for Jesus in every detail, we should connect the main point of an Old Testament

---

c. In Chapter 5, we'll also discuss connections to Jesus' person and character. See the section titled, "Remember Jesus in Your Application."

passage to these three truths about Jesus. The message of the whole Bible is a unified message summarized in these three truths from Luke 24:46–47.

For example, the call of Abraham in Genesis 12:1–9 is about how God chose one man to be the focal point of blessing for the whole world. What's the connection to Jesus? His message is *for every nation* (Galatians 3:8–9).

When God asked Abraham to sacrifice his only beloved son (Genesis 22), he was showing both Abraham and us how *the Messiah had to die and rise from the dead* (Hebrews 11:17–19).

When innocent Daniel was tossed into the lion's den and came out unharmed (Daniel 6), he foreshadowed *the Messiah's death and resurrection.*

When Moses and Solomon wrote laws and proverbs, God was revealing his high standards. He had to expose our inability to perform so we might learn to *repent of our sins and be forgiven.*

Where do we see Jesus in Genesis 1? Although passages like John 1:1–5 and Hebrews 1:1–3 clearly identify Jesus as the creator of all things, we must see him also as redeemer. When God calls humanity to illuminate, shape, and fill the earth in his name, he establishes a standard we can't possibly keep perfectly. But Jesus can, and repentant sinners will find forgiveness in him.

Paul has Genesis 1 in mind as he proclaims the

gospel—good news—to "all creation under heaven" in Colossians 1.

- The good news of illumination: Jesus, the fullness of God, radiates God's glory (Colossians 1:19–20) and delivers us from darkness into light (Colossians 1:12–13).

- The good news of shaping: Jesus, the head of the body, created all things and holds them together; he rules and subdues all things that in everything he might be preeminent (Colossians 1:16–18).

- The good news of filling: Jesus, the firstborn of all creation, fruitfully multiplies in the earth, reconciling you by his death and presenting you holy and blameless before God (Colossians 1:15, 21–22).

- Jesus, the image of the invisible God, brings redemption, the forgiveness of sins (Colossians 1:14–15). And you, previously alienated and hostile, must continue in the faith, not shifting from the hope you have heard (Colossians 1:21–23). With Christ in you, you have hope of glory (Colossians 1:27). You can now walk worthy of the Lord, pleasing him, bearing fruit, and knowing God (Colossians 1:9–10).

Moses called Israel to illuminate, shape, and fill the earth in God's name. They would never perfectly fulfill this mandate; they desperately needed the Messiah's calling to repentance and forgiveness. So also we should shine the truth of the gospel, shape our world for God's glory, and fill the earth with more disciples. Again, while we can't perfectly *meet* this goal, our call is to continue persevering in faith in *pursuit* of this goal. Jesus died and rose to make that pursuit possible (Matthew 28:18–20).

Let me conclude this chapter with a brief word about interpreting the New Testament. The three truths of Jesus I listed above (from Luke 24:46–47) apply just as much to the New Testament as to the Old Testament, and we miss the point when we miss that connection. Here are three examples.

1. *All four Gospels* magnify and climax on *Jesus' death and resurrection*; they present Jesus as much more than a role model. Thus, Jesus' healing miracles often show Jesus "trading places" with sufferers in order to save them (Matthew 8:14–17); Jesus is not only an example of social justice but also a savior to the ostracized and the unjust.

2. *Much of Acts and many epistles* elaborate on how Jesus' message is *for all nations*. Since Jews and Gentiles were brought together in one body, any person of any gender, race, or class can freely receive Jesus' forgiveness and unite with his body.

3. *Instructional passages*—like the fruit of the
   Spirit (Galatians 5:16–26) or the "love chapter"
   (1 Corinthians 13)—don't make us into more
   righteous, more acceptable, people; they show
   us what happens to *people whose sins are
   forgiven* because they have trusted in Christ
   and received his Spirit.

As you interpret, don't stop until you see Jesus in every
passage.

Your Turn

1. How does the main point of Genesis 2:4–25 show Jesus?
2. You may photocopy the following worksheet (or download a larger
   version from www.knowableword.com/resources) to help with
   interpretation.

INTERPRETATION WORKSHEET #2

Text: _____

1. Answer Questions from the Text

2. Context, Flow of Thought, & Main Point

3. Connection to Jesus

- Death and resurrection, or

- Need for repentance and forgiveness, or

- Proclamation to all nations

Four

From Inertia to Application

Hearing, Doing, and Changing

Vihaan was squirming. I didn't want to make him uncomfortable, but something bigger than his comfort was at stake.

A native of India, Vihaan had come to the U.S. to get a degree in business administration. He had joined my Bible discussion group to learn more about Western culture, and over the course of a semester he had come to understand Jesus' claim to be God.

"Do you think the Bible's account of what Jesus said is untrustworthy?" I asked.

"No, I think we can trust it."

I tried again: "Do you think Jesus was lying?"

"No, he's probably telling the truth."

"Do you think it would be worth it to give your life to Christ?"

"Of course. Eternal life with God would be wonderful."

"Then why not trust him and follow him?"

"I could never do that. I came here to get my degree

so I could return home and manage our family's business. If I became a Christian, I would lose everything. My parents would disown me. I would lose my future. I would lose my position and my respect. I can't do that."

Vihaan and I remained friends for the next three years, but after this conversation, he wouldn't discuss the Bible or Jesus any further.

Vihaan had no problems with observation or interpretation. But he missed application and so missed the freedom and life found in knowing God.

Why Should Christians Apply the Bible?

Explaining why Christians should apply the Bible is almost like explaining why lovers should kiss or why children should open birthday presents. Good things delight the soul, and true delight can't be captured in a numbered list. There's something magical and beautiful in the diligent application of Scripture, so I wish I could simply say, "It's more fun than a prepaid Amazon shopping spree," but this important question warrants at least four concrete answers.

Christians should apply the Bible because we know God. Though we still have sin, we don't love it like we used to. We have a new allegiance, and the lover of our souls offers a promising alternative to our old habits, values, and patterns of thinking. "But now that you have come to know God, or rather to be known by God, how can you turn back again to the weak and worthless elementary principles of the world, whose slaves you want to be once more" (Galatians 4:9)?

Christians should apply the Bible because we are known by God. He knew us before we ever knew him, and he has vowed to make us more like Jesus. "For those whom [God] foreknew he also predestined to be conformed to the image of his Son" (Romans 8:29a).

Christians should apply the Bible because we are free from sin's dominion. We're not stuck in the old way of doing things. We don't have to keep hurting ourselves and the people we love. We're free to do what God wants us to do, which is always the best thing we could do. "But thanks be to God, that you who were once slaves of sin have become obedient from the heart to the standard of teaching to which you were committed, and, having been set free from sin, have become slaves of righteousness" (Romans 6:17–18).

Christians should apply the Bible because... we are Christians! A static life is inconsistent with true faith. According to 1 John, we'll know we have eternal life by three pieces of evidence: confessing Christ, loving others, and keeping God's commandments. These proofs don't imply sinlessness—John expects us to repent often and be forgiven (1 John 1:8–2:2)—but they do mean our lives should change over time to better reflect what God wants for us.

> And by this we know that we have come to know him, if we keep his commandments. Whoever says "I know him" but does not keep his commandments is a liar, and the truth is not in him, but whoever keeps his word, in him truly the love of God is perfected. By this we may know that we are in him: whoever says he abides in him ought to walk in the same way in which he walked (1 John 2:3–6).

Christians may have a good sense of why they should apply the Bible to their lives but still struggle to do so. For those who simply don't know *how*, I'll give plenty of suggestions to get you started. For those who can't find the motivation, something more is needed. That something is the gospel.

Gospel-Motivated Application

A few years ago I attended a marriage conference taught by Paul Tripp, author of *What Did You Expect?*[19] Tripp spoke the Word of God powerfully, and he paved the road of application with dozens of vivid personal stories. Few stories made him look good; most were about his epic failures as a husband. During a break, I overheard an attendee ask Tripp how he could be so frank and vulnerable in public. His answer exemplified gospel-motivated application: "Jesus died for me, so I have nothing left to prove." Here was a man living and leading others as though he really believed Romans 8:1: "There is therefore now no condemnation for those who are in Christ Jesus."

Here's the magic. Here's the beauty. God offers you your freedom. He knows you better than you know yourself, and he'll make you more useful than you dreamed possible. He wants what's best for you, and he makes his best available to you. You have nothing left to prove, so you're free to admit you were wrong, take God at his Word, and do your best, by grace, to live his way.

When people ask why we should apply the Bible and go through the hard changes of sanctification, I wonder why on earth we'd want to stay the same.

Your Turn

1. What motivates you to apply the Bible?
2. What prevents you from applying the Bible?

The Greatest Enemy of Application is Inertia

Physical science defines inertia as "a property of matter by which something that is not moving remains still and something that is moving goes at the same speed and in the same direction until another thing or force affects it."[20] Inertia keeps a stationary boulder still, and inertia keeps a moving boulder barreling on in the same direction. Moving the still boulder, or redirecting the moving boulder, requires force.

In this metaphor, you and I are the boulders, and the application of Scripture is the force needed to overcome our inertia, thus changing us from one state to another. Sounds like work, doesn't it? It is. Boulders aren't easily redirected, and neither are our stubborn souls. Done right, application of Scripture will always be a challenge. We should expect this challenge to take two forms.

The challenge of movement. Inertia keeps us in the same place, but the Lord wants to move us. We can grow comfortable with how things are, but through the Word, the Holy Spirit moves us toward what might be. He pushes, pulls, nudges, convicts, cajoles, challenges, batters, and compels. He gets us moving toward Christ. Thus the ignorant person gets a clue. The indifferent person begins to care. The idle person gets to work.

The challenge of redirection. Inertia keeps us moving in the same direction, but if it's the wrong direction, the Lord wants to turn us toward him. We generally like to keep doing what we're doing, but through the Word, the Holy Spirit adjusts our trajectory and redirects our path. He disciplines, directs, bumps, pursues, pesters, collides, invites, and overwhelms. He alters our course to face Christ. Thus the angry person learns to love. The argumentative person learns to listen. The manipulative person learns to let go.

Hearers and Doers

Application is terribly inconvenient. It makes us doers of the Word, unlike inertia, which encourages us to remain merely hearers of the Word. As James writes:

> But be doers of the word, and not hearers only, deceiving yourselves. For if anyone is a hearer of the word and not a doer, he is like a man who looks intently at his natural face in a mirror. For he looks at himself and goes away and at once forgets what he was like. But the one who looks into the perfect law, the law of liberty, and perseveres, being no hearer who forgets but a doer who acts, he will be blessed in his doing (James 1:22–25).

James takes issue, not with hearing, but with hearing and not doing. Hearing is good; it means that you "receive with meekness the implanted word, which is able to save your souls" (James 1:21). But hearing without doing is inconsistent. God's perfect law promotes a life of liberty, but obstinate inertia is an imprisoning insanity—Jesus likened it to building a beach hut in a hurricane zone (Matthew 7:26–27).

Of course, at any given moment I can faithfully be a doer of the Word in some areas of life while being content only to hear the Word in other areas. Hearer-only and hearer-plus-doer are not absolute categories, but tendencies we all carry within ourselves as people who apply the Word of God imperfectly. In any given instance or moment, insofar as I honor God with my lips, I live as a hearer. But insofar as I *also* repent and believe the gospel I live as a doer. For example:

- To go to church is to hear. To practice the truth that was preached is to do.

- To love theology is to hear. To attempt to persuade others about theology, yet without quarreling, is to do.

- To identify what you've learned speaks of hearing. To identify how you've changed speaks of doing.

- Asking questions of Scripture is about hearing. Acting on the right answers is about doing.

- To talk about obeying the civil authorities is proof of hearing. To refuse to conceal taxable income is proof of doing.

- A sense of conviction over sin is about hearing. To make changes is about doing.

- To know who Jesus is, is to hear. To cooperate actively with God in the daily process of being conformed into his image, is to do.

When the founders of the United States declared their independence from Great Britain, they based their actions on self-evident truths, including the creator's endowment of all men with certain inalienable rights.

Among those immutable rights was the pursuit of happiness. What is the pursuit of happiness? According to an 1884 Supreme Court ruling, it is "the right to pursue any lawful business or vocation, in any manner not inconsistent with the equal rights of others, which may increase their prosperity or develop their faculties, so as to give them their highest enjoyment."[21]

The threat that King George posed to the colonies wasn't so much a threat of sadness as a threat of maintaining the status quo. He wanted things to continue as they had been, with the colonies under his thumb, paying well, and unable to improve their lives and communities. The signers of the declaration knew that the greatest threat to their pursuit of this kind of happiness was the inertia of the status quo.

From a pragmatic and political perspective, that Supreme Court ruling does a pretty good job of defining the pursuit of happiness. But of course God offers us so much more. Peter tried to describe the happiness that Christ offers to those who persevere in the faith, rejecting a spiritually unprofitable inertia and cooperating with God in redirecting the boulder. You get the feeling that Peter was almost at a loss for words when he called that kind of happiness, "joy that is inexpressible and filled with glory" (1 Peter 1:8).

That's some serious joy. The joy that comes with spiritual change is worth fighting for. Let's learn how.

Your Turn

1. In what areas of your life are you most often a doer? In what areas are you typically only a hearer?
2. What are some of the reasons you end up staying still or simply maintaining your current direction?
3. How might you overcome this inertia?

The Challenging Art of Producing Change

Jesus commanded his disciples to go and make disciples of all nations (Matthew 28:19). From this fact, we can conclude that the Bible must apply to any person in any culture at any point in time. (The X diagram in Chapter 3 visually represents this versatility.) Thus, while a passage of Scripture won't have infinite *interpretations*, it can have an essentially infinite number of *applications.* But therein lies a problem, for you and I aren't naturally fans of a large number of applications. We much prefer a small number of cookie-cutter solutions to whatever challenges present themselves. We want life to be simpler than it actually is, so our approach to application often tends toward legalism.

On the one hand, application on the personal level must get very specific so our lives can change. Yet on the other hand greater specificity increases the risk of legalistic generalization—as if I should expect you to change in all the same ways I need to change and by the same set of techniques. After all, an application that makes sense for one person might not make sense for another. For example, Jesus has no problem calling some people to leave their family (Mark 1:19–20, Luke 9:59–60) while instructing another to return to them (Mark 5:18–19). Let us remember that application is the work of both God and the Christian: he who *works his good pleasure in you* expects you to *work out your own salvation* (Philippians 2:12–13). So don't make the mistake of trying to take over from God once you think you have discovered some secret technique that somehow makes unnecessary the one who grants you every breath, and without whom you can do nothing.

In teaching people how to apply the Bible, then, it's important to provide both universal principles (questions to ask, categories to consider, etc.) and particular examples (of how other Christians have applied the passage). Some people feel directionless without the former, while others feel hopeless without the latter. As we go, we must be careful not to set our hope in the principles (independent of God's grace), and we must not naively clone the examples (independent of godly wisdom). For the remainder of this chapter and on into the next I will explain the principles, and I'll close Chapter 5 with personal examples.

Two Directions for Application

To begin with, I recommend building application upon the passage's main point. While you can certainly apply minor points, working from the main point gives your application more teeth; it focuses you on what God considers most important.

When I've got the main point, I generally begin my application with two simple questions: *How do I need to change?* and *How has God called me to influence his world?* The first question focuses on internal change, and the second question focuses on external influence. These two "directions" of application come straight from Jesus.

The Great Commandments: How Do I Need to Change?

First, Jesus expects *us* to change. Consider this summary of how to obey God's commands:

> And one of them, a lawyer, asked him a question to test him. "Teacher, which is the great commandment in the Law?" And he said to him, "You shall love the Lord your God with all your heart and with all your soul and with all your mind. This is the great and first commandment. And a second is like it: You shall love your neighbor as yourself. On these two commandments depend all the Law and the Prophets." (Matthew 22:35–40)

Jesus takes "all the Law and the Prophets"—the entirety of God's instruction—and boils it down to two things: love God and love your neighbor. These two loves characterize the progressive work of God in your life, and they encapsulate God's will for you. These are the Great Commandments.

The Great Commission: How Does God Call Me to Influence His World?

Second, Jesus expects us to change *the world*. Consider this summary of how to build God's kingdom:

> Now the eleven disciples went to Galilee, to the mountain to which Jesus had directed them. And when they saw him they worshiped him, but some doubted. And Jesus came and said to them, "All authority in heaven and on earth has been given to me. Go therefore and make disciples of all nations, baptizing them in the name of the Father and of the Son and of the Holy Spirit, teaching them to observe all that I have commanded you. And behold, I am with you always, to the end of the age." (Matthew 28:16–20)

Jesus employs "all authority in heaven and on earth" — his divine resurrection power — to this end: empowering his people to win more people in his name. This mission characterizes the progressive work of the church through the ages, and it encapsulates God's will for the world. This is the Great Commission.

The Great Commandments and the Great Commission show two "directions" in which we can apply any passage of the Bible: inward and outward. We can become a more Christ-like people with greater love for God and people (inward application), and we can become a more Christ-like people with greater influence in the world (outward application). The Bible produces change both *in us* and *around us*.

Let's practice on Genesis 1.

Remember the main point of this passage: God's creative work sets a pattern for human dominion of the earth, so humanity fulfills its potential when it *illuminates, shapes*, and *fills* the earth in God's name. Let's apply this passage to the two "directions" of change.

Internal change. Starting from the main idea of Genesis 1, how can you grow and manifest a deeper *love for God and people*?

- How can you *illuminate* the darkness? (for example, by replacing lies with truth)

- How can you *shape* the formlessness? (for example, organizing your life in a way that protects your time with the Lord and serves others better)?

- How can you *fill* the emptiness? (for example, being more productive overall)

- Where have you failed to image God in these ways?

- How can you trust Jesus more fully in these areas?

- How can you become more like Jesus in these areas?

External influence. Starting from the main idea of Genesis 1, whom should you serve or lead, and how can you help them to become better stewards of their domains?

- How can they *illuminate* the darkness?

- How can they *shape* the formlessness?

- How can they *fill* the emptiness?

- Where have they failed to image God in these ways?

- How can you encourage them to trust Jesus more fully in those areas?

- How can you be a better influencer for Jesus?

Each of these general questions should lead to more specific points of action that fit your particular situation. How should you change? How has God called you to influence his world? And how does Christ's death and resurrection make it possible?

All the Law and the Prophets, and Christ's mission on earth, can be summed up by these two directions for application.

Your Turn

Get more specific: how does Genesis 1 and 2 instruct you to change and be changed?

FIVE

Head, Heart, Hands

Three Spheres of Change

In the previous chapter we set the stage for application. It wasn't so much about application itself as it was about helping us prepare for application. We need to understand why application is important, why we can have hope for it in Christ, and how we can understand the two basic directions of change (internal and external). Now it's time to bring application down to a more practical level.

Remember those boulders we discussed in the previous chapter? To overcome inertia I must apply force + direction. I can't move a boulder merely by facing it in the direction I want it to go. I must also apply some pressure before I'll see any change. This chapter is about the right kind of pressure.

One simple way to apply effort (pressure) and provoke change (overcome inertia) is by considering three spheres: head, heart, and hands. These spheres represent three aspects of human life where we can both change and be changed. As we will see, Paul suggested these three spheres of application when he taught his protégé Timothy how to use the Bible.

The head represents everything we think and believe. Head application means being a *hearer* of the Word. This sphere involves thinking God's thoughts after him and believing what he says. In this sphere, we meditate on the attributes and nature of God the Father, Son, and Holy Spirit. We identify the lies we believe and replace them with the truth. We remember the gospel, as Paul suggested to Timothy, with our heads:

> But as for you, continue in what you have *learned* and have firmly *believed*, knowing from whom you *learned* it and how from childhood you have been *acquainted* with the sacred writings, which are able to make you *wise for salvation* through faith in Christ Jesus (2 Timothy 3:14–15).

The heart represents who we are. Heart application is the first and foundational part of being a *doer* of the Word. This sphere involves walking in righteousness, desiring the Lord above all, and showing godly wisdom and selfless character. As the seed of the gospel takes deep root, we set aside our old loves and instead begin to love God and others. The gospel, now internalized, shapes our hearts according to the Lord's own righteousness. "All Scripture is breathed out by God and profitable for teaching, for reproof, for correction, and for *training in righteousness*" (2 Timothy 3:16).

The hands represent everything we do. Hands application is the second part of being a *doer* of the

Word. This sphere involves laying aside our old patterns of selfish behavior, imitating the Lord and his ambassadors, and becoming more effective at building God's Kingdom. Thus, the gospel begins to bear fruit. "that the man of God may be *complete,* equipped for *every good work*" (2 Timothy 3:17).

God wants to produce change in all three spheres—head, heart, and hands—but many people naturally incline toward only one or two. The trick of application is to address all three areas without imbalance.

Your Turn

Which of the three spheres do you find easiest or most difficult? Why?

Apply the Bible to Your Head

If you skip the head and go right to the heart or hands, you might have good intentions while doing all the wrong things. Have you experienced a compassionate person with trite answers for your suffering? Or a sacrificial person with baseless and unsatisfying ideas about God? Have you been that person? Knowing God through his Word will change your thinking, such that your loving and serving can be effective.

- Consider 1 Timothy 4:16, where Paul urges Timothy to keep a close watch on himself *and on his teaching*, for by so doing he would save both himself and his hearers.

- Consider Ephesians 4:22–24, where Paul describes Christian maturity as a three-step process. 1) Put off the old self. 2) *Be renewed in the spirit of your mind.* 3) Put on your new self.

- Consider Matthew 22:46, where Jesus is too wise to be ensnared by sneaky questions.

Maybe you want to change your thinking and receive the mind of Christ. But how, you ask, does one do this? Here are three uncomplicated steps:

1. Identify what you think.

2. Identify what God wants you to think instead (especially about his attributes, his character, and his world).

3. Begin thinking God's thoughts.

For example, how could we apply the main point of Genesis 1 (illuminate, shape, fill) to the head?

Let's go inward first. To help us track how this section applies to the head, I will italicize the relevant words. Do you usually *think* you're the sovereign master of the universe, or do you *remind yourself* that God's in charge? Do you *believe* you'll be most satisfied by relaxing in front of the TV (or clamping down on your kids, or working longer hours) or by fulfilling God's purpose for you in the world? What worldly *ideas* about leadership have you swallowed (such as imbalanced approaches to self-esteem, empowerment, tolerance, or authenticity), and how could you be more *influenced* by God's character, words, and deeds? Each

mind shift requires you to believe that God is simulta-
neously powerful and good; thus, he's worth imitating,
and he'll accomplish his purpose despite your failure.

Let's go outward as well. What do you *think* about
other people? Are they worthy of the respect and dig-
nity befitting them as made in the image of God, even
when they're disagreeable or infuriating? If so, you'll
believe that all people are worthy of acceptance and
goodwill. You'll also *believe* that anyone can change—
and that all people can be saved, even the most unlikely
candidates. Some people *think* they could never lead
others, while others excuse their spiritual despotism.
Where do you fall on the spectrum, and what is God
calling you to?

I'm sure these few paragraphs don't exhaust the
applications you can make to your head, but what do
you… *think*?

Your Turn
What "head" applications arise from your study of Genesis 2?

Apply the Bible to Your Heart

If you stop with head application, you've been a hearer
of the Word without being a doer of it. Have you met
a professor who taught the Bible but seemed cool to-
wards God? Or a theologian who was good at being
right but not so good at being patient, gentle, or hum-
ble? We must apply the Bible to the head, but we must
also be careful not to miss the heart.

God resolved long ago to conform his people to the image of Jesus (Romans 8:29), which means he wants us to be like him. He doesn't want us only to think like him. He doesn't want us only to act like him. He wants us to become like him. Therefore, as you apply the Bible to your life, you should always ask, "What kind of person does God want me to be?" You can tackle this question in several different ways:

- What do you *desire* or *value*, and how can you adopt Jesus' desires or values where you suspect yours and his don't match up?

- What ungodly *character traits* should you turn from, and what Christ-like character traits can you imitate instead?

- In what areas do you tend to *rely* on your performance, and how can you rely more on Christ's performance?

- What are your greatest *hopes*? Is your bucket list too small compared to the Lord's desires?

- Are yours the kind of *heart attitudes* others should seek to acquire? Why or why not, and what will you do about it?

Let's practice again with Genesis 1. How might we apply its main point to our hearts?

Inward application. God wants us to illuminate and shape the world for his glory. Are you *content* letting darkness and chaos reign in your heart? Do you *love* God's kingdom in something like the way Christ does? How can you better align your *dreams* with God's purpose? Christ left the perfection of heaven to associate with us and change the world; what comforts can you become *willing* to relinquish so you can be more industrious for the Lord? How can you gain the *desires* you need to better handle your responsibilities? What *character* traits will qualify you for more leadership?

Outward application. God wants to grow his kingdom on earth. He desires all people to be saved and to come to the knowledge of the truth. Are you increasingly joining with God in that *desire*? Would people who know you say they see some reflection of the Lord Jesus in your *apparent heart attitudes*? As you parent your children, rub shoulders with your co-workers, or participate in your small group, do you have a *desire* to win people to the vision of building Christ's kingdom?

Our hearts must change before our lives can change. And once our hearts change, we're ready to apply the Bible to our hands.

Your Turn

What "heart" applications arise from your study of Genesis 2?

Apply the Bible to Your Hands

Christians should be the hardest workers, the most delightful neighbors, and the most trustworthy companions. Why? Not because we need anyone to be impressed with our performance, but because…

- We've been bought with a price and now get to honor God with our bodies (1 Corinthians 6:20).

- We have a new master, and we work for him, not (ultimately) for any human supervisors (Colossians 3:23–24).

- We know what it's like to be forgiven much (Luke 7:47–48).

- Jesus is making all things new (Revelation 21:5), not only in our spiritual lives but also through our relationships, reputation, and work ethic.

Then why do outsiders so often see Christians as lazy, condescending, irritable, and ignorant? On the one hand, lots of people may call themselves Christian but aren't, so this doesn't help the overall reputation of actual believers. But even among people of real faith we are, as a general rule, nothing too special—and the Bible says exactly that! God frequently chooses to adopt into his family the powerless and unimpressive so that, as he works through us to change the world, he receives greater glory (1 Corinthians 1:26–31).

So while Jesus is in the business of changing people, he has to start somewhere. He has to start with you and me—and that leaves plenty of room for improvement, doesn't it? Nevertheless, over time, he makes the unlovely lovely. He takes the weak and gives them his strength. He makes the poor rich in him, and the ignorant wise in him. If you follow him, he'll shape you into something useful and guarantee you a part in the greatest drama in the universe.

This means that your application of the Bible must hit your hands. The Bible will prepare you to learn skills (practical, interpersonal, spiritual) you may have never imagined you could acquire. It will instruct you and train you in fresh ways so you can become a skilled laborer for the kingdom of God.

What does it look like to apply the Bible to your hands? Let's practice once again by applying the main point of Genesis 1.

Inward application. Because of God's free mercy, we can confess lazy *choices*, and because of God's empowering grace, we can make more industrious *choices*. Illuminating the darkness might mean reminding yourself of the gospel or *memorizing* Scripture. Shaping the formlessness could mean *cleaning* your bedroom or *tracking* your budget. Filling the emptiness could mean *having* children, *completing* a project, or *doing* laundry. Remember, there is no end to the applications you could make, and there are no cookie-cutter answers. The key question is: how does God want you to steward your life this week, this month, this year—a life he bought with his Son's precious blood?

Outward application. Perhaps you could… find a way to *share* your hope in Christ with your neighbors… *teach* your children to work hard and serve Jesus… *avoid* complaining about your church's problems and instead contribute to the solutions… *train* co-workers to be more effective and help the company succeed. God's grace compels you to mold this world for his glory.

When application has transformed your mind and conformed your heart to Christ, it will change you visibly.

Your Turn

What "hands" applications arise from your study of Genesis 2?

The Application Matrix

Hearers of the Word apply the Bible to the head—doers of the Word *also* apply the Bible to the heart and hands. In other words, those who trust in Christ persevere in faith, awaiting the final day when Jesus resurrects head, heart, and hands to immortality and glory. Until then, they work out their salvation day by day, learning to love God, love others, and influence the world for Christ.

The Application Worksheet found in this chapter

APPLICATION WORKSHEET

Text: _____

	Inward	Outward
Head		
Heart		
Hands		

(also downloadable from the resources page at www.knowableword.com) might help when application doesn't come easily. You don't have to fill in every box in every Bible study, but be sure to hit every box over time lest the following pitfalls ensnare you:

- **Too much inward focus produces self-centered living.** Push your application outward, and consider how to be more effective at serving and influencing others for Christ.

- **Too much outward focus produces hypocritical living.** Don't ask others to do what you're not willing to do yourself. Don't ask them to change unless you're willing to change first.

- **Too much head focus produces overly theological application.** God cares about what you think and believe, but he also cares about your character and obedience.

- **Too much heart focus produces overly pietistic application.** God cares about who you are, but your character should flow out of your thinking and into your obedience.

- **Too much hands focus produces overly ethical application.** God cares about what you do, but he also cares about your thinking and character.

The six boxes on the worksheet's matrix are not magical. The point is not to fill in boxes, but to become like

Christ. So as you work on the boxes, remember Jesus and get specific.

Your Turn

1. Which boxes on the matrix come most intuitively for you?
2. Which boxes require the most effort from you?
3. Find some people to help you implement your applications from Genesis 1 and 2.

Remember Jesus in Your Application

Paul, the great apostle to the Gentiles, was about to die. He had fought the good fight, run the race, and kept the faith. The crown of righteousness awaited him, and he was more than ready for it. But first he had to give his chief protégé a few parting instructions, which included the following:

> Remember Jesus Christ, risen from the dead, the offspring of David, as preached in my gospel, for which I am suffering, bound with chains as a criminal. But the word of God is not bound! Therefore I endure everything for the sake of the elect, that they also may obtain the salvation that is in Christ Jesus with eternal glory. (2 Timothy 2:8–10)

"Remember Jesus Christ." Why did a mature Christian leader say something so apparently elementary? How could Timothy possibly forget about Jesus? Isn't Jesus the reason he became a pastor? Isn't Jesus the one who put the "Christ" in "Christianity?"

But there was nothing elementary about Paul's reminder. Paul insisted on emphasizing what we so often ignore: that the most dangerous tendency for Christians is to forget Jesus. We must resist this tendency even when we study the Bible.

After we have been Christians for a while, most of us gradually slip into a pattern where, when it comes to living the Christian life, we begin to rely more on our discipline than on Jesus. We delight in Jesus' salvation from our past sins, but now we live as though it's up to us to please God. Having begun by the Spirit, we drift into seeking perfection through the flesh.

How does this affect the way we treat the Bible? At first, we come to it as a book of hope for sinners who can find eternal life in Jesus. But over time we begin treating the Bible as a list of rules or doctrines, and we bludgeon others and ourselves into following the rules or regurgitating the doctrines, either out of guilt or duty. Thus we bind the Word of God and burden believers with ethical, pietistic, or doctrinal chains.

So let us now focus on the importance of remembering Jesus—especially his merciful character—in our application.

When studying a Bible passage, you might make an interpretive connection *to* Jesus, but your work is not yet done. Your application must also derive *from* Jesus and his saving work. Only by remembering Jesus will your heart be strengthened to action.

In other words, nothing motivates like grace. You can't drum up greater faithfulness from the inside. You must be broken by God's unbelievably high standard, and you must rest in Jesus' death in your place and obedience on your behalf. Only then will you walk the straight and narrow and have something worth imparting to a new generation. Only then can you say with Paul Tripp, "I have nothing left to prove."

I'll give an example. My church once hired a young rookie pastor. He was a fine preacher, and he'd been well trained to preach Jesus from the text. His first week on the job, he got in the pulpit and preached with boldness and clarity.

But he made a few mistakes. He stumbled over his words. He got nervous and said a few things that were slightly naïve. After the service, discouraged by his failures, he expected us elders to hammer him. After all, preaching is important business. You can't mislead God's sheep or you're in big trouble. As we got ready to evaluate the sermon together, he braced himself for some well-earned criticism.

While we neither ignored his mistakes nor approved of them, we reminded him that Jesus had already died for them. Because the gospel is true, this freshly ordained minister was free to make mistakes. I conveyed to him the life-changing advice I had received from my high school band director: "If you make a mistake, make it a big one." I encouraged him to make more mistakes in the future. I preferred that he give it his all, making a few mistakes in the process, than that he hold back out of fear of imperfection. He was free to live his calling as a preacher with confidence that he was accepted by God and already approved.

Seminary prepared him to *interpret* the Bible with a focus on Jesus, but only persistent faith would train him to *apply* it with a focus on Jesus.

So, let's study (and especially apply) the Bible with such great confidence in Jesus that we can "sin boldly," as Martin Luther once advised his student Philip Melanchthon:

> Be a sinner, and let your sins be strong (sin boldly), but let your trust in Christ be stronger, and rejoice in Christ who is the victor over sin, death, and the world. We will commit sins while we are here, for this life is not a place where justice resides. We, however, says Peter (2 Peter 3:13), are looking forward to a new heaven and a new earth where justice will reign.[22]

Your Turn

1. How will you remember Jesus when you fail to apply Genesis 1 and 2?
2. How will you remember Jesus when you succeed?

Be Specific in Your Application

Finally, your application will flutter uselessly in the wind of life unless you nail it down. Don't settle for broad principles; make concrete action steps. Beware the trap of high-minded platitudes.

"How are you today?"

"Fine. How are you?"

"What did you think of the sermon?"

"It was pretty good. I learned a lot."

"What is God teaching you?"

"I should have a better prayer life…[or] I need to love my family…[or] I'd like to be a witness to my coworkers."

We hear God's Word all the time, but we often respond so generally that our lives rarely change. And since God wants to change specific people in specific ways, we should be specific in our application.

The apostle John wrote a letter to churches infiltrated by false teachers. These slick celebrities liked to spout self-serving clichés like, "We know God," and "We love God"—but like a sub-surface infection, they threatened the church's vitality. True believers were second-guessing themselves and their assurance of eternal life because these teachers claimed to have critical inside knowledge unavailable to the masses. And in the face of reproof, these teachers wouldn't change.

At the beginning of the letter, John takes them on. He exposes these elitist, self-righteous dissemblers for what they are: "If we say we have no sin, we deceive ourselves, and the truth is not in us" (1 John 1:8). In other words, if we refuse to acknowledge that we are sinners in a *general* way, we are utterly deceived. There is no special status with God by which we can become sinless this side of glory. Anyone who claims otherwise understands neither themselves nor the Scriptures.

But notice which error John exposes next: "If we say we have not sinned, we make him a liar, and his word is not in us" (1 John 1:10). In other words, when confronted with a *specific* sin, anyone who covers it up, shifts the blame, or denies it declares God to be a liar and his Word to be false.

John is saying that those who know God's Word will acknowledge two things—I have *sin* (a sin nature), and I have *sinned* (specific instances). Thus, it's not enough to trust in Christ to forgive your sin if you're not willing to admit to the details. This means that your application of Scripture must be specific. Starting from the general and moving to the specific: this is how change works. Platitudes aren't enough. Generalities will not carry you where you need to go.

Here are a few ideas to help you move from general principles to specific applications.

Know your next steps. Don't be satisfied with your application until you've identified specific steps you can take to address the issue. When you close the Bible and walk away, what will you do to put application into practice? How will you remember these lessons in the midst of temptation?

Make your progress measurable. How will you

know if you did the application or not? "Pray more" is not measurable. "Pray more than twenty minutes a day in an undistracted setting" *is*. Make your goals measurable.

Put off and put on. Think of application as a process of stopping certain things (sinful patterns) and starting other things (godly patterns). Put off the old self, and put on the new self. You won't stop a particular sin until you've found a viable, satisfying alternative for it. For example, don't just stop lusting; find ways to serve people.

Don't be lame. I know this point is subjective, but perhaps I've attended too many Bible studies that tried to pump me up with clichés such as, "Let go and let God… Christianity is not a religion but a relationship… do it for the glory of God." Slogans like these may have roots in the truth of Scripture, but they won't change anything unless you add specifics.

God's knowable Word smashes like a jackhammer and repairs like a blowtorch. It rips us apart and puts us back together. It identifies exactly what is wrong with the world: me and you. It shows us the solution: Jesus. It gives us hope that we can break the patterns of brokenness and replace them with more life-giving options. Let it speak to the details of your life.

Your Turn

How can you make your application of Genesis 1 and 2 more specific to your life right now?

My Application

Here's a snapshot of the details of my life. I'll offer current personal application from my study of Genesis 1. Please hear me, though. I'm not saying these are the applications *you* should be following. Maybe they are; maybe they aren't. I'm just doing this to give you an example of clear, specific application targeted against the inertia in one man's life in a particular season.

Main Point

When I apply Genesis 1 to my life, I first remind myself of the main point:

> *God's creative work sets a pattern for human dominion of the earth, so humanity fulfills its potential when it illuminates, shapes, and fills the earth in God's name.*

Inward Application

Next, I consider how the main point compels me to change. As I consider my responsibility to image God by shaping his world, I realize that I have a very hard time with house projects. I'm not a guy who enjoys home improvement; I'd rather find a creative way to get my left earlobe caught in a paper shredder. But since it's clear God has entrusted me with this domain to steward, the next step is for me to get even more specific about my beliefs, values, and behaviors.

Head. When faced with the prospect of a home

improvement project, I can easily be tempted to fall back into my habit of believing I will always be bad at home improvement and can never enjoy it. As application, I can choose to *confess* the truths that I'm a steward of this house and that God actually hasn't given me a bum deal. He didn't stick me with a discontented, former-civil-engineer wife to drag me down with her list of project bids. No, he gave me a ministry partner who understands better than I do how to make our home a center of family life and hospitality. I must *change my thinking* when I sense my disgruntlement taking over. Do I *believe* God is omnipotent? Do I *believe* God is good? Do I *see* my house as a gift or a liability? Is it mine, or is it God's? I must repent of the mistaken, self-serving belief that God cannot change me in this area. I must stop using it as an excuse to avoid stepping out in faith and doing the right thing. I must replace this false belief with one that is more biblically true: I can change. By God's grace, I can learn to be more handy, and even to enjoy it.

Heart. I will *praise God* for my house; I *won't complain in my heart*. When I'm *tempted* to despair over the unending decay and brokenness, I will *trust* that the Lord is still at work. I will replace my bitterness, fear, and love of pleasure with contentment, joy, and faith in the one who has promised to build his house (in part by me working on my own house)! Because Jesus' bodily house was struck down and raised in three days, I can be *assured* that God will make all things new. I'll look with *hope* toward the new heavens and new earth, where we can build and maintain good things for God's glory without such drudgery.

Hands. Then I'll get to *work*. I won't wait for my wife to recruit helpers for house projects; I'll *do it* myself. I'll *speak* with her this week to make sure we agree on how to move forward with the next home-improvement project. I *won't complain* when she promotes a new project; I will *thank her* for helping me. If I fall back into complaining, then instead of blaming circumstances or excusing myself, I'll confess, change, and *grab my tools.* I can do all this because Jesus died for me.

Outward Application

I begin by remembering that God has called me to be fruitful by shining gospel light to all nations. My struggle in this area is to believe God will actually win the lost. I can too easily imagine that people who aren't already "in" will ever be. My love of a comfortable status quo hinders my ability to recruit people to the Lord. When I am reminded of this big-picture problem, I am then prepared and motivated to get more specific about my beliefs, values, and behaviors.

Head. I may not *believe* God can win outsiders, but that's simply not true. He does it all the time. I will *read* Exodus, Esther, and Acts in the next thirty days to remind myself of this truth. In addition, I will ask my wife and closest friends to reprove me when I'm withdrawing from people. I won't hide behind the label "introvert" to justify my self-centered choices.

Heart. I will ask God to *shape my heart* to reflect his own. Because judgment is coming, I will *put on* compassion and hope. I will *pray* for specific people by name. I will *remember* how Christ rescued me from my self-destructive idolatry, and I will *desire* this rescue for the names on my list.

Hands. I'll *subscribe* to a blog or newsletter that tells missionary stories.[23] I will *invite* Neighbor X to our small group. I will *invite* Neighbor Y to church. I will *follow up* on my conversation with Neighbor Z about parenting, listening, and hope for the future, and I will *find a way* to work Christ into the discussion. I will *call* Relative Q to see how he's doing. I will *talk* to my wife to discuss what other opportunities lie before us.

With this list of commitments, the boulder just might get moving in the right direction. Of course, words on a page don't equal life change, but with these words, I have a concrete idea of specific things I can go and do.

Now, I must be honest: I rarely come away from Bible study with a list of applications this long. Usually, I grab one or two specific ideas and try to run with them. But for this chapter I wanted to give lots of examples. May the Lord work his good pleasure in us as we work out our salvation.

Six

The Unity of the Whole

Correlation across Texts

We have tried to teach our children to work hard. We speak of God as a hard worker and a kind master who sees everything and calls us to obey with all our hearts. We have even watched ants together, observing their ways. One day, however, my wife found our 5-year-old son sitting idle while he was supposed to be cleaning the bedroom he shares with his brother. She proceeded in her motherly way, "You need to help your brother clean up. It's not kind for you to sit there and let him do all the work." And then, from amid the room's wreckage came a groan almost too deep for words, a biblically informed groan from the diligent but overtaxed brother, "He does that all the time. He's like an Egyptian."[24]

God wants us to make connections in his Word. Stories illustrate instructions. Poems put an experiential face on theology. Passages in one section often expand on ideas presented in another section, producing a more complete picture of God's truth. This process of connecting passages is called correlation.

Understanding the Whole Bible

The Bible consists of sixty-six different books, written by dozens of people across millennia. The Bible is also one book, written by one author (God the Holy Spirit), conceived in eternity and executed in history.

In OIA Bible study, we focus primarily on the diversity of Scripture. Each author of each passage has a unique point to make. We read each text in its context to figure out its main point and connect it to Jesus. Different cultures and different generations will draw different applications from the same main points, as they should. It's beautiful when we see God's knowable Word connecting with any person in any culture at any time.

However, we shouldn't neglect the unity of the Scripture. God the Holy Spirit spoke through each of these human authors. He strategically unraveled the stories and laws and poems and letters in just the right way to reveal the Lord Jesus to the world.

Thus, after studying a passage of Scripture, we should connect what we have learned to the rest of Scripture. This process is called correlation.

For example, Genesis 1 teaches about God's pattern of creation and his mandate to humans to imitate it. But it's not the only passage that speaks of God's creation or image. It's not the only passage that gives purpose to human existence. In fact, if we treat Genesis

1 as though it has the whole truth about the creation, we'll come away with a pretty thin perspective.

We can miss the fact that God's creation work was full of wisdom and delight (Proverbs 8:22–31). We can grow disillusioned by how often the created world changes, forgetting that God, who superintends it all, ever remains the same (Psalm 102:25–28). We can find ourselves trying in the *wrong* way to be like God (Genesis 3:5). We can make unwarranted distinctions between "good" creations and "bad" creations (1 Timothy 4:3–5). We can lose hope by thinking of this world as if it's all there is, and thus despair over our sin and minimize the reality of the new heavens and earth to come, where righteousness dwells (2 Peter 3:11–13).

Stephen understood correlation when he spoke to the Jewish rulers in Acts 7. He didn't focus on just one Bible passage, but he connected many passages together to show how the technically religious had always rejected the truly godly.

The author of Hebrews understood correlation when he wrote of the intricate connections between priest, temple, and sacrifice—and how the whole system finds its fulfillment in Jesus.

John understood correlation when he wrote his climactic book of signs (Revelation). He fused all the imagery of the Bible into a dense letter written to encourage persecuted believers in the Roman province of Asia. John was so skilled at smooth correlation that many people miss it today. We too often read Revelation in the dubious light of current "end-times" events and futurist speculations, *instead of* in the light of the other sixty-five books of the Bible, as John intended (Revelation 1:1–3).

In short, correlation is the process of constructing a coherent theology from the Scripture. We shouldn't pit one passage against another. Rather, let's work to understand how they all fit together. As we do so, we get to know the Lord who made himself known in the Scripture.

Three Tips for Healthy Correlation

Correlation is not the same thing as cross-referencing. Cross-referencing is what we do when we surf the Bible as though it were YouTube. We read one passage, which links to another one, which links to another one, which links to another one, which links to another one, world without end, amen.

Unfortunately, random cross-referencing rarely produces much insight into any of the texts. It certainly takes a lot of time, which produces some satisfaction. But it doesn't help us to know God. It's like speed dating, giving an impression of activity without much intimacy.

How do we correlate effectively while avoiding the dangers of unhelpful cross-referencing? What will help us make solid connections and correlations between passages?

The Order of Correlations

When I'm studying a passage from the Bible and I feel stuck (because the meaning isn't coming to me as quickly or intuitively as I'd prefer), I'm tempted to short-circuit interpretation by cross-referencing. But this puts me in danger of making a poor connection, since *I can't judge the strength of the connection until I understand the passage at hand*.

When I feel stuck, the answer is usually to go back and observe better. Or I need to ask and answer additional interpretive questions. Either way, I should take a stab at the main point *before* I attempt correlation with other passages.

Cross-references certainly have a purpose, but you can't assume they have been selected to help illuminate the main idea of a passage, which is the true goal of Bible study. For example, one of my study Bibles has a cross-reference on Genesis 1:26 that leads to Ephesians 4:24. There's a clear verbal connection between "Let us make man in our image, after our likeness" (Genesis 1:26) and "Put on the new self, created after the likeness of God in true *righteousness* and *holiness*" (Ephesians 4:24). Another cross-reference leads to Colossians 3:10, "Put on the new self, which is being renewed in *knowledge* after the image of its creator."

While all three passages *mention* the image or likeness of God, the danger lies in letting ideas from a cross-referenced passage influence your thinking about the main idea of the primary passage. If I take ideas of righteousness, holiness, and knowledge from Ephesians and Colossians, and read them back into Genesis 1:26, I will probably miss the main point of the Genesis passage: to explain God's image through the pattern of illuminating, shaping, and filling. Only *after* discovering the meaning of Genesis 1 am I ready to connect it to the passages in Ephesians and Colossians.

Don't let correlation distract you from careful interpretation of a text on its own terms. But once you've interpreted, go ahead and correlate.

The Purpose of Correlations

In former generations, Bible scholars commonly sought to harmonize parallel passages. They would take a story, such as the feeding of the 5,000 (told in Matthew 14, Mark 6, Luke 9, and John 6) and combine the many details into a single account. Sometimes people would even preach or comment *from* the harmonized text rather than from any of the original texts.

If you like old commentaries, you may know what I mean. John Calvin, for example, didn't write commentaries on Matthew, Mark, or Luke. He wrote one commentary called *Harmony of the Evangelists*, synthesizing the texts of these three books.

Calvin had some good points, but harmonization

inevitably misses the fact that Matthew, Mark, and Luke often had *different primary points* to make, even when recounting the same event.[d] Accordingly, contemporary interpretive theory has shifted such that scholars usually comment on individual books and not on "harmonies." This goes not only for the Gospels but also for Samuel, Kings, and Chronicles; for Kings and Isaiah; and for Exodus, Leviticus, Numbers, and Deuteronomy (with respect to laws, not events).

At best, harmonizing may dull our ability to observe. For example, you may have heard of the "rich young ruler." But guess what? The phrase doesn't appear in your Bible. Matthew 19 speaks of a "young man," Mark 10 calls him a man who had "great possessions," and Luke 18 calls him a "ruler" who was "extremely rich." We think of him as the "rich young ruler" only because we've been instructed out of an approach that focuses on harmonizing related biblical accounts.

At worst, however, harmonizing can actually obstruct interpretation. For example, if we import John's "bread of life" idea into every account of Jesus feeding the 5,000, we may obscure the unique main points of Matthew, Mark, or Luke.

When we do connect or correlate passages, our main purpose should not be to harmonize but to

---

d. For a case study, visit www.knowableword.com/category/bible-study/feeding where I explore the main points of each Gospel's account of the feeding of the 5,000.

illuminate. For example, when Peter proposes in Matthew 17:4 to erect three tents on the mount of transfiguration, without the parallel accounts his words might appear to be innocent, thoughtful, or sacrificial. Yet Mark 9:6 says Peter was terrified, and Luke 9:33 says he didn't know what he was saying. These passages clarify Peter's thoughts and prevent us from reading his words in Matthew the wrong way.

Correlation can get tricky sometimes. But it will be easier if, before connecting passages, you consider the purpose of the connection. Don't flip to another passage merely for more *details*; flip to find necessary *light*.

The Nature of Correlations

While internet search engines and Bible software make it easier than ever to look up every instance of a particular word or phrase, we must be careful not to treat the words of Scripture like a code to crack. We shouldn't treat words, or even phrases, as though they have only one meaning or always have a particular slant to them. We know that the meaning of an English word isn't always found exclusively in the word itself but in the word's usage in a particular context. Then why do we sometimes assume the opposite when it comes to Scripture? Language is far more flexible than is apparent in the average word study.

Word connections *can* be quite helpful when it comes to people or place names (for example, if you're reading Philippians, you might search for *Philippi* to get more background on it from Acts). But for general vocabulary? Not so helpful. Though Genesis 1:3, Ezekiel 8:17, and Matthew 11:30 all use the word *light*, they're not necessarily talking about the same thing.

Here's a better way forward: connect ideas, not just words. Study each passage in context and grasp its main point. Then look for other passages that address a similar topic or idea. *Then* connect them to get a fuller picture of the idea.

As you correlate, correlate well. You'll know God's Word better, and you'll grow closer to the Lord himself, passage after passage, day after day. After all, the whole Bible is about him.

Your Turn

1. How does Genesis 1 contribute to your theology of God, people, and the world?
2. What other passages in Scripture provide complementary truths on these topics?
3. What does Genesis 2 add?

Appendix
You Are Approved!

Most of us can learn to use our Bibles far, far better. While this book provides a basic introduction to the OIA method—enough to get you started on a life of much more fruitful Bible study—it only begins to scratch the surface.

Jonathan spent a year learning OIA Bible study skills and then helped his small group re-focus on the Bible. Before that, the group would bounce from one study guide to the next, believing themselves incapable of handling the Scripture without expert guidance. But Jonathan suggested they simply read a book of the Bible and discuss it. So they did, and I believe they're still doing it.

Dorothy received six months of OIA training in adult Sunday school and in the process contracted a contagious love for Scripture. This elderly widow had served faithfully in the church for decades. She believed the gospel and never grew out of her need to hear it preached, but she had grown accustomed to being told what to think and do as a Christian. Learning how to study God's Word herself was like reconnecting with an old friend.

Ming came to know Christ, learned to study the

Bible, and wanted to share her new faith with her father, a communist official back in China. She didn't have access to any specialized resources, so she simply asked him if he'd like to read and discuss the Gospel of John with her weekly. Armed with a webcam, a broadband internet connection, and the sword of the Spirit, she introduced him to the Word made flesh.

I hope you see that the OIA method of Bible study is more than a good idea; it's a tool to help you rightly handle the Word of truth. And as you rightly handle the Word of truth, you get to know the Word made flesh, who is the truth.

You Are Now Approved to Study the Bible

Sometimes people avoid Bible study because they feel unqualified, but I'm here to tell you that you're ready. You've graduated. You're accepted for the position. And while you did just finish a simple training course in how to study the Bible, that's not why you're ready. Your fundamental qualifications go much deeper.

Hear Paul's exhortation to Timothy: "Do your best to present yourself to God as one approved, a worker who has no need to be ashamed, rightly handling the word of truth" (2 Timothy 2:15). Here at the end of this book, I want to inspire you with this passage and reiterate your irrevocable credentials to study the Word of God.

But first, let's make sure we avoid a crucial mistake.

In verse 15, Paul is not saying, "Present yourself to God *in order to win approval from him.*" One thing all Christians have in common is that God already approves of us *in the most important sense of the word*—we have been accepted by God because of the finished work of Jesus Christ. We therefore can and should come to him, and to his Word, on the basis of that acceptance and approval.

Besides, who could carry that burden? Sinners who think they need to gain God's approval through their performance eventually stop trying to get it. They keep failing, so they give up.

But Paul is doing more in this passage than reminding Timothy that he is a precious and approved child of God. It's obvious from the context that Paul is exhorting Timothy to teach the Bible well. And this is where the concept of approval in verse 15 takes on another level of meaning.

Paul is essentially saying two things to Timothy in this verse. He says them to us, too.

- First, let us come to the Word of God as men and women qualified to do so because God approves of us, has adopted us into his family, and has sealed us with the indwelling Holy Spirit of promise. This is our primary qualification for studying the Word of God and finding his revealed truth within it.

- Second, let us recognize that, on the basis of this fundamental and irrevocable approval, we should zealously dig into God's Word with the tools we have available, confident that he is eager to teach us as we seek to become ever more skillful at handling the Word of truth *in ways that meet with his approval.*

Don't study the Bible to get approved. Study it because you're already approved. Jesus died and rose to qualify you for a position close to God. Study the Bible and see this message of grace on every page.

Miss the message of grace, and you'll no longer handle the Word rightly. Does this mean you can never make mistakes? Of course not. But if you trust in Christ, then you're forever approved, and you're free to keep trying each day to get it right.

AUTHOR

Peter Krol has taught the Bible since 1996 both as a collegiate missionary with DiscipleMakers (www.dm.org) and as an elder in both Presbyterian and Independent churches. He's trained dozens of people to study the Bible. Many of them now train others who, in turn, have begun training a third generation. With each new year, he reads nothing but the Bible until he finishes the Bible — not because it makes God any happier with him, but because it makes him happier with God in Christ.

ACKNOWLEDGMENTS

Though I've been teaching OIA for a decade and a half, I never would have written it down in this book were it not for my DiscipleMakers teammates who helped me start the Knowable Word blog (www.knowableword.com): Tom Hallman, Joel Martin, Brian Roberg, and David Royes. Also, the Senior Leadership of DM and the elder board of Grace Fellowship Church were incredibly generous with time and counsel for the project. It's my privilege to minister God's Word alongside of you.

Thanks to all who read early drafts of the manuscript and offered useful counsel: Alison Amaismeier, Jeremy Amaismeier, Ian Busko, Jenny Carrington, Mike Chartowich, Lyn Chartowich, Andy Cimbala, Bill Dripps, Bonnie Dripps, Lincoln Fitch, Matt Geiger, Ben Hagerup, Dave Kieffer, Skeets Norquist, and Gene Williams. Special thanks to Jed Stalker and Joe Smith for providing painstaking editorial advice to a fledgling writer, and to Kevin Meath for employing his inscrutable editorial magic to make this book so much stronger.

Many thanks also to Dan Miller and Holly Howden for the graphics within this book, and to Caleb Olshefsky for the invaluable concept work on the second edition's cover design.

Finally, I offer my deepest thanks to my wife, Erin. You are the prettiest and smartest editor an author could wish for. The Spirit of Christ may have given me some decent ideas from time to time, but he gave me you to make them sing.

ENDNOTES

1. The classic text is Robert A. Traina, *Methodical Bible Study* (Grand Rapids: Zondervan, 1952). Seminaries call it the "historical-grammatical method of Bible interpretation." Some more popular approaches call it "inductive Bible study." Others call it COMA: Context, Observe, Meaning, Apply (David Helm, *One-to-One Bible Reading*, Sydney, Australia: Matthias Media, 2011), SOAR: Survey, Observe, Analyze, Respond (Denis Haack, *A Practical Method of Bible Study for Ordinary Christians*, Ransom Fellowship, 2008), or the Swedish Method: a light bulb, a question mark, an arrow (http://matthiasmedia.com/briefing/2009/01/the-swedish-method/, accessed 3/24/2014), but the substance is the same.

2. Phrases taken from DiscipleMakers Core Value: Scripture (www.dm.org).

3. From personal email correspondence with DiscipleMakers President Emeritus Bill Dripps.

4. David Dorsey, *The Literary Structure of the Old Testament* (Grand Rapids: Baker academic, 1999). Especially helpful are the Introduction, Chapter 2: "Literary Units," Chapter 3: "Arrangement of Units," and Chapter 4: "Structure and Meaning."

5. *ESV Study Bible* (Wheaton, IL: Crossway, 2008), p 40.

6. http://www.golfdigest.com/golf-instruction/swing-sequences/2011-04/evolution-of-tigers-swing, accessed 3/24/2014.

7. Gordon D. Fee and Douglas Stuart, *How to Read the Bible for All Its Worth* (Grand Rapids: Zondervan, 2009), Kindle locations 204–206.

8. Leland Ryken, *A Complete Handbook of Literary Forms in the Bible* (Wheaton, IL: Crossway, 2014) Kindle location 303.

9. For more information about various faithful Christian approaches to Genesis 1, see Vern Poythress, *Christian Interpretations of Genesis 1* (Phillipsburg, NJ: P&R, 2013) or David Hagopian, ed., *The Genesis Debate* (Toronto: Crux Books, 2000).

10. I am indebted to the Charles Simeon Trust (www.simeontrust.org) and its Workshops on Biblical Exposition that introduced me to the concept and value of text type as a crucial element to observe.

11. Douglas Wilson, *Wordsmithy* (Moscow, ID: Canon Press, 2011), p 104.

12. Ludwig Wittgenstein, *Philosophical Investigations*, § 112.

13. http://www.brainyquote.com/quotes/quotes/g/geddylee304949.html, accessed 3/26/2014.

14. http://www.landofwisdom.com/author/thomas-carlyle/page17.html, accessed 3/26/2014.

15. http://www.biography.com/tv/classroom/bio-of-the-month-albert-einstein, accessed 3/27/2014.

16. Robert A. Traina labels these three categories as definitive, rational, and implicational questions.

17. Bruce Waltke, *Genesis: A Commentary* (Grand Rapids, MI: Zondervan, 2001), p 64.

18. Or visit www.knowableword.com/resources for a comprehensive list of Old Testament quotes in the New Testament.

19. Paul Tripp, *What Did You Expect?* (Wheaton: Crossway, 2010).

20. http://www.merriam-webster.com/dictionary/inertia, accessed 4/1/2014.

21. *Butchers' Union Co. v. Crescent City Co.*, 111 U.S. 746, 757 (1884).

22. Letter 99, Paragraph 13. Erika Bullmann Flores, tr. from: *Dr. Martin Luther's Saemmtliche Schriften*, Dr. Johann Georg Walch, ed. (St. Louis: Concordia Publishing House, n.d.), Vol. 15, cols. 2585–2590.

23. Possibly Voice of the Martyr's newsletter at http://www.persecution.com.

24. The child had in mind the enslavement of the Hebrews by the ancient Egyptians as recorded in Exodus.

Sowable Word: Helping Ordinary People Learn to Lead Bible Studies

Peter Krol | 168 pages

Discover the surprising glory and astounding fruit borne from leading a Bible study.

bit.ly/Sowable

Who Am I?
Identity in Christ

by Jerry Bridges | 91 pages

Jerry Bridges unpacks Scripture to give the Christian eight clear, simple, interlocking answers to one of the most essential questions of life.

bit.ly/WHOAMI

The Ten Commandments of Progressive Christianity

Michael J. Kruger | 56 pages

A cautionary look at ten dangerously appealing half-truths.

bit.ly/TENCOM

Endorsed by Collin Hansen, Kevin DeYoung, Michael Horton

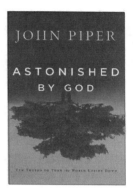

Astonished by God
Ten Truths to Turn the World Upside Down

John Piper | 192 pages

Turn your world on its head.

bit.ly/AstonishedbyGod

The Company We Keep
In Search of Biblical Friendship

Jonathan Holmes
Foreword by Ed Welch | 112 pages

Biblical friendship is deep, honest, pure, tranparent, and liberating. It is also attainable.

bit.ly/B-Friend

Preparing for Marriage
Help for Christian Couples

John Piper | 86 pages

As you prepare for marriage, dare to dream with God.

bit.ly/prep-for-marriage

Don't miss these fully inductive Bible studies for women from Keri Folmar!

Loved by churches. Endorsed by Kristi Anyabwile, Connie Dever, Gloria Furman, Kathleen Nielson, and Diane Schreiner.

Six volumes and growing! **Visit bit.ly/DITWStudies**

10 weeks

Joy! (Philippians)

10 weeks

Faith (James)

10 weeks

Grace (Ephesians)

11 weeks

11 weeks

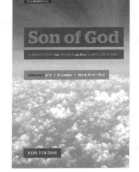

Son of God (Gospel of Mark, 2 volumes)

9 weeks

Zeal (Titus)